Joys of Jell-O®

GELATIN DESSERT

THE STORY OF JELL-O ®
....AND WHY IT GREW

Jell-O Gelatin first grandly shimmered its way into American dining rooms in 1897. Just how many brands in your kitchen go back over 70 years? Very few, you can be sure, and fewer still have continued to grow in popularity the way Jell-O Gelatin has each year.

Just why is this? Well for one thing, housewives liked it so much they turned their imaginative attention to Jell-O, invented all sorts of ingenious recipes using it, and contributed them to the very first Jell-O Gelatin recipe book—50 years old now if it's a day. Since then, this wonderfully light, wholesome dessert with its luscious fresh fruit taste has grown to an exciting array of refreshing flavors and become America's all-time family favorite.

Joys Of Jell-O includes lots of familiar old recipes and lots of new ones, too. Hundreds of recipes for desserts, salads, relishes, and confections chosen from the thousands in existence. Some are plain and very simple to make; some are glorious as the 4th of July, but they are still pretty simple to make.

Jell-O Gelatin's long-time popularity comes from many good things. Its lightness is one — a big one. Jell-O Gelatin is so light it seems to make any meal sit a little lighter. Its fresh fruit taste, so much like the fruit that inspired it, is utterly satisfying. And it's easy to fix in all kinds of ways — some we'll wager that have never entered your mind.

The bounty of Jell-O doesn't end with its lightness, good taste, convenience, and versatility. Jell-O Gelatin is nutritious and low in calories, just 81 calories per half-cup serving. It sits as lightly on your conscience as it does on top of any meal. You can add fresh vegetables or fruit, or even a marshmallow or two, and eat and eat.

ANSWERS TO SOME QUESTIONS

How in the world do you unmold Jell-O so it looks like the molds in the advertisements? The last chapter of this recipe book will clear up this question. It will also tell you how to whip, flake, and cube Jell-O Gelatin. And that's not all. It's full of time-saving tips and tricks on how to make Jell-O. So why not have some for dinner tonight? Whether you eat lavishly or just a little ... there's always room for Jell-O.

General Foods Kitchens

(From top to bottom)

RAINBOW CAKE (page 24)

PINEAPPLE CHEESE DESSERT (page 15)

RING-AROUND-THE-FRUIT (page 23)

HAWAIIAN DESSERT

A fluffy dessert made in a blender is ready to serve quickly.

1 can (1 lb. 4½ oz.) crushed pineapple
1 package (3 oz.) Jell-O Lime or Lemon Gelatin
½ cup milk
¼ teaspoon almond extract
¾ cup crushed ice

Drain pineapple, reserving ¾ cup syrup. Bring syrup to a boil; add Jell-O Gelatin, stirring until gelatin dissolves. Combine pineapple and milk in an electric blender; blend well. Add gelatin mixture, extract, and ice. Mix thoroughly in blender. Pour into dessert dishes. Chill until set, about 1 hour. Makes about 3 cups, or 6 servings.

PASTEL DESSERT

A creamy, smooth blend of three convenient mixes that's very versatile.

1 package (3¼ oz.) Jell-O Vanilla Pudding and Pie Filling
1 package (3 oz.) Jell-O Gelatin (any fruit flavor)
2½ cups water
1 envelope Dream Whip Whipped Topping Mix

Combine Jell-O Pudding, Jell-O Gelatin, and water in a saucepan. Cook and stir over medium heat until mixture comes to a *full* boil and is thick and clear. Remove from heat. Chill until slightly thickened. Meanwhile, prepare whipped topping mix as directed on package.

Thoroughly blend the prepared whipped topping into the chilled mixture. Spoon into individual sherbet glasses or a 1-quart mold or serving dish. Chill until firm. Unmold. Makes about 4 cups, or 6 to 8 servings.

Pastel Pie: Prepare Pastel Dessert, pouring mixture into a cooled baked 9-inch pastry shell.

Desserts

For parties, picnics, and family meals—

Roast beef and carrots and things like that are all very well, but kids, husbands, and guests never get quite as worked up over them as they do over dessert. With Jell-O Gelatin they can get as excited as they please, because it's so light, wholesome, and nourishing. Here we've included all manner of desserts made with Jell-O Gelatin—elegant ones for special occasions, simple ones for everyday, and some you can even pack in a cooler for outings.

LADYFINGER DESSERT

For special occasions, form a flag, heart, bell, or other symbol with the whipped cream on this red dessert.

    1 package (3 oz.) Jell-O Cherry
      or Black Cherry Gelatin
    1 cup boiling water
    1 cup cold water
    ¼ teaspoon almond extract
    8 ladyfingers, separated and
      cut in half crosswise
    ¼ cup chopped maraschino
      cherries (optional)
    Sweetened whipped cream or
      prepared Dream Whip Whipped
      Topping
    ⅓ cup Baker's Angel Flake or
      Premium Shred Coconut

Dissolve Jell-O Gelatin in boiling water. Add cold water and almond extract. Pour ¾ cup into a 9-inch pie pan. Chill until slightly thickened. Insert ladyfingers around sides of pan. Chill until set, but not firm. Chill remaining gelatin until very thick; then whip until fluffy—see directions on page 84. Fold in cherries. Pour over gelatin in pan. Chill until firm. Top with whipped cream and coconut. Makes about 3 cups, or 6 servings.

CARDINAL PEAR MOLD

An easy way to glamorize inexpensive canned pear halves.

    1 package (3 oz.) Jell-O Cherry
      or Black Cherry Gelatin
    1 cup boiling water
    1 can (1 lb.) pear halves
    ½ teaspoon grated orange rind
      (optional)
    ⅛ teaspoon ground ginger
    ⅛ teaspoon salt

Dissolve Jell-O Gelatin in boiling water. Drain pears, measuring syrup. Add water to make ¾ cup, if necessary. Add syrup, orange rind, ginger, and salt to gelatin. Pour into individual molds. Chill until firm. Unmold and serve with pear halves. Makes 2 cups gelatin, or 4 servings.

MINT JULEP DESSERT

The traditional Southern beverage has inspired a cool, minty dessert.

    1 package (3 oz.) Jell-O Lime
      Gelatin
    1 cup boiling water
    1 can (8½ oz.) sliced pineapple
    4 drops each mint and pepper-
      mint extracts
    Whipped cream or prepared
      Dream Whip Whipped Topping
    4 maraschino cherries

Dissolve Jell-O Gelatin in boiling water. Drain pineapple, measuring syrup and adding water to make ¾ cup; add to gelatin. Stir in extracts. Chill until firm. Flake with fork and spoon into 4 sherbet glasses. Top with a slice of pineapple, a dollop of whipped cream, and a cherry. Makes 1¾ cups gelatin, or 4 servings.

PASTEL POUND CAKE

A moist, tender cake that's flavored with fruit flavor gelatin.

    1 package white or yellow cake
      mix
    1 package (3 oz.) Jell-O Gelatin
      (any fruit flavor)
    ¾ cup water
    ½ cup salad oil
    4 eggs, unbeaten

Empty cake mix into large bowl. Add remaining ingredients. Beat 3 minutes, or until smooth and creamy. Pour batter into 10-inch tube pan that is lined on bottom with paper. Bake in moderate oven (350°F.) 50 to 55 minutes. Cool in pan 15 minutes. Then remove from pan and cool on cake rack. Sprinkle with confectioners' sugar, if desired.

NOTE: This cake may also be baked in the following paper-lined pans: two 9x5x3-inch loaf pans 40 to 45 minutes; one 13x9x2-inch pan 40 to 45 minutes; two 9-inch layer pans 30 to 35 minutes; two 8-inch layer pans 35 to 40 minutes; or one 9-inch tube pan 60 to 65 minutes.

Lemon-Glazed Cake: Prepare Pastel Pound Cake, baking it in a 13x9x2-inch pan. Cool in pan 15 minutes. Gradually blend ⅓ cup lemon juice into 2 cups sifted confectioners' sugar. Add 2 tablespoons melted butter and 1 tablespoon water. Remove cake from pan; place on rack. Punch holes through cake with toothpick. Pour on glaze, allowing it to run into holes. Place on serving platter.

QUICK FRUIT DESSERT
(Pictured on page 77)

You can make this fruit mold just an hour or so before serving.

   1 package (3 oz.) Jell-O Gelatin
      (any fruit flavor)
   1½ cups boiling water
   1 package (10 oz.)
      Birds Eye Fruit*
   ¼ cup chopped nuts (optional)
Use Birds Eye Mixed Fruit, Strawberries, Red Raspberries, or Peaches.

Dissolve Jell-O Gelatin in boiling water. Add frozen fruit and stir gently until fruit thaws and separates—gelatin may begin to thicken. Add nuts. Spoon into dessert dishes. Chill until set—about 30 minutes. Makes 3 cups, or 6 servings.

Quick Fruit Sauce: Prepare Quick Fruit Dessert, adding ½ cup cold water. Serve on cake squares or creamy puddings. If sauce becomes too thick upon standing, place over hot water until thin enough to pour. Makes about 3⅓ cups.

RASPBERRY CHANTILLY

Peach jam is the surprise addition to whipped raspberry gelatin.

   1 package (3 oz.) Jell-O Black
      Raspberry or Raspberry Gelatin
   ¼ teaspoon salt
   1 cup boiling water
   1 cup cold water
   1 cup whipped cream or prepared
      Dream Whip Whipped Topping
   ½ cup peach jam

Dissolve Jell-O Gelatin and salt in boiling water. Add cold water. Chill until very thick. Then whip the gelatin until fluffy—see directions on page 84. Stir in whipped cream or prepared whipped topping and jam. Pour into serving dishes or individual molds. Chill until firm. Serve with additional whipped cream or prepared whipped topping, if desired. Makes about 5½ cups, or 8 servings.

MARSHMALLOW PARFAITS

Even the children will enjoy making a dessert as easy as this one.

   1 package (3 oz.) Jell-O Gelatin
      (any fruit flavor)
   1 cup boiling water
   1 cup cold water
   1 cup miniature or diced
      marshmallows

Dissolve Jell-O Gelatin in boiling water. Add cold water; chill until very thick. Whip ⅔ cup of the gelatin until fluffy—see directions on page 84. Spoon about half of the clear gelatin into parfait or slender 5-oz. glasses. Top with marshmallows, whipped gelatin, and remaining clear gelatin—in that order. Chill until firm. Makes about 4 cups, or 6 to 8 servings.

SPICED FRUIT CUPS

A little cinnamon adds flavor to a jellied fruit mold.

   1 package (3 oz.) Jell-O Gelatin
      (any fruit flavor)
   ¼ teaspoon cinnamon
   1 cup boiling water
   1 can (1 lb. 1 oz.) fruit cocktail

Dissolve Jell-O Gelatin and cinnamon in boiling water. Drain fruit, measuring syrup; add cold water to make 1 cup. Stir syrup into gelatin. Chill until very thick. Fold in fruit. Pour into serving dishes or individual molds. Chill until firm. Serve with prepared Dream Whip Whipped Topping or whipped cream, if desired. Makes about 3 cups, or 6 servings.

ORANGE FROST

A double orange treat that is refreshing after or between meals.

1 package (3 oz.) Jell-O Orange Gelatin
1 cup boiling water
1 pint orange sherbet
1 cup sweetened whipped cream or prepared Dream Whip Whipped Topping
⅛ teaspoon ground ginger (optional)

Dissolve Jell-O Gelatin in boiling water. Add the sherbet by spoonfuls, stirring until melted. Then beat until frothy. Spoon into sherbet glasses or a 1-quart mold. Chill until firm. Garnish with whipped cream to which ginger has been added. Makes about 3 cups, or 4 to 6 servings.

FROSTY MANDARIN DESSERT

A cooling combination of orange gelatin, orange sherbet, and oranges.

2 packages (3 oz. each) or 1 package (6 oz.) Jell-O Orange Gelatin
2 cups boiling water
1 can (11 oz.) mandarin oranges
1 pint orange sherbet, softened

Dissolve Jell-O Gelatin in boiling water. Drain oranges, measuring syrup; add water to make 1 cup. Add to gelatin. Chill until slightly thickened. Blend in sherbet and mandarin oranges. Pour into a 1-quart mold. Chill until firm. Unmold. Makes about 4½ cups, or 8 servings.

NOTE: If desired, substitute 1 cup cold water for the syrup mixture and 1 cup drained diced fresh orange sections for the mandarin oranges.

LAYERED CHEESECAKE

Fruit flavor gelatin serves as a delicious contrast to cream cheese.

1 package (3 oz.) Jell-O Black Raspberry, Black Cherry, or Raspberry Gelatin
1 cup boiling water
1 cup cold water
1 cup graham cracker crumbs
¼ cup butter, melted
1 package (3 oz.) cream cheese, softened
2 tablespoons light cream
¼ cup confectioners' sugar

Dissolve Jell-O Gelatin in boiling water. Add cold water. Chill until syrupy. Meanwhile, mix cracker crumbs and butter. Line a 9x5x3-inch loaf pan with wax paper, letting it extend as 2-inch tabs at either end. Then press crumb mixture into bottom of pan. Blend cream cheese and light cream; mix in confectioners' sugar. Spread over crumb mixture. Then pour gelatin carefully over cream cheese. Chill until firm. To serve, run point of knife between sides of pan and cake; then lift cake from pan with paper tabs. Remove paper and place on serving plate. Slice. Makes about 6 servings.

BANANA FLUFF

A light dessert containing two popular fruits plus marshmallows.

1 package (3 oz.) Jell-O Raspberry or Strawberry-Banana Gelatin
Dash of salt
1 cup boiling water
1 can (8¾ oz.) crushed pineapple
1 banana, mashed
1 cup finely cut or miniature marshmallows

Dissolve Jell-O Gelatin and salt in boiling water. Drain pineapple, measuring syrup. Add cold water to make ¾ cup; add to gelatin. Chill until very thick. Then whip until fluffy—see directions on page 84. Fold in pineapple, banana, and marshmallows. Pour into a 1½-quart mold or serving dish. Chill until firm. Unmold; serve with a fruit sauce, if desired. Makes about 6 cups, or 8 servings.

For 16 to 18 servings: Use two 3-oz. or one 6-oz. package Jell-O Gelatin and double the remaining ingredients. Pour into two 1½-quart molds.

BASIC BAVARIAN

Versatile—use it plain, add fruit or cubed gelatin, or layer two flavors.

1 package (3 oz.) Jell-O Gelatin (any fruit flavor)
¼ cup sugar
1 cup boiling water
¾ cup cold water or fruit juice
1 envelope Dream Whip Whipped Topping Mix or 1 cup whipping cream

Dissolve Jell-O Gelatin and sugar in boiling water. Add cold water. Chill until slightly thickened. Then prepare the topping mix as directed on package or whip the cream; stir 1½ cups into gelatin until blended. Pour into a 1-quart mold or bowl, or 6 to 8 individual molds or serving dishes. Chill until firm, or freeze until firm—about 4 hours. To serve, unmold and garnish with remaining whipped topping or whipped cream. Makes about 3½ cups, or 6 servings.

NOTE: If desired, 1 cup sliced or diced fresh or drained canned or frozen fruit may be folded into Bavarian before molding. The drained fruit syrup may be used in the gelatin.

Bavarian Pie: Prepare Basic Bavarian, measuring and setting aside ¼ cup gelatin before adding whipped topping, if desired. Pour Bavarian mixture into a cooled baked 8-inch pie shell; chill until set, but not firm. Then glaze top with reserved gelatin. (If reserved gelatin is too stiff to spread, place container in a pan of hot water until gelatin is syrupy.) Chill until firm. Garnish with remaining whipped topping.

Rainbow Bavarians: Prepare Basic Bavarian twice, using a different flavor of Jell-O Gelatin in each (such as strawberry in one and lime in the other). Then layer the Bavarians in a 2-quart mold or bowl, parfait or other tall glasses, or serving dishes. Chill until firm. Unmold and garnish with remaining whipped topping. Makes 12 servings.

Two-Tone Desserts: Prepare 1 package (3 oz.) Jell-O Gelatin (any fruit flavor) as directed on package; pour into 10 to 12 individual molds or sherbet glasses, only partially filling each. Chill until set, but not firm. Meanwhile, prepare the same or another flavor of Basic Bavarian; pour over set gelatin in molds. Chill until firm. Unmold and garnish with the remaining whipped topping. Makes 10 to 12 servings.

Crown Jewel Bavarian: Prepare cubes of Jell-O Gelatin (see page 85). Before cutting cubes, prepare Basic Bavarian. Then cut ½-inch cubes and fold into Bavarian. Pour into a 1½-quart mold or 10 to 12 individual molds or serving dishes. Chill until firm. Unmold; top with remaining whipped topping. Makes 10 to 12 servings.

COCONUT BAVARIAN

Coconut-lovers will praise the hostess who serves them a cool, fluffy dessert containing their favorite flavor.

> **1 package (3 oz.) Jell-O Gelatin (any fruit flavor)**
> **1 cup boiling water**
> **¾ cup cold water**
> **¾ cup whipping cream or 1 envelope Dream Whip Whipped Topping Mix**
> **⅔ cup Baker's Angel Flake Coconut**

Dissolve Jell-O Gelatin in boiling water. Add cold water. Chill until slightly thickened. Whip cream or prepare whipped topping mix as directed on package; blend 1½ cups into gelatin. Add coconut. Spoon into 1-quart

mold or serving dishes. Chill until firm. Unmold. Garnish with remaining whipped topping, if desired. Makes about 4 cups, or 6 to 8 servings.

DE LUXE BAVARIAN

Frozen raspberries make it extra delicious, as well as simple to prepare.

> **1 package (3 oz.) Jell-O Orange or Raspberry Gelatin**
> **¼ cup sugar**
> **Pinch of salt**
> **1½ cups boiling water**
> **1 package (10 oz.) Birds Eye Red Raspberries**
> **1 envelope Dream Whip Whipped Topping Mix or 1 cup whipping cream**
> **16 ladyfingers, split**

Dissolve Jell-O Gelatin, sugar, and salt in boiling water. Add raspberries, stirring until berries separate. Chill until slightly thickened. Prepare the topping mix as directed on package or whip the cream; stir 1½ cups into gelatin until blended. Line a 1½-quart mold with ladyfingers. Pour Bavarian mixture into mold. Chill until firm. To serve, unmold and garnish with remaining whipped topping. Makes about 4 cups, or 6 to 8 servings.

GRAPE JUICE BAVARIAN

It's refreshing, but also rich and satisfying. Try it soon.

> **1 package (3 oz.) Jell-O Concord Grape or Lemon Gelatin**
> **¼ cup sugar**
> **1 cup boiling water**
> **1 cup grape juice***
> **1 cup whipping cream or 1 envelope Dream Whip Whipped Topping Mix**

*Or use ½ cup grape juice and ½ cup water.

Dissolve Jell-O Gelatin and sugar in boiling water. Add grape juice. Chill until slightly thickened. Whip the cream or prepare the whipped topping mix as directed on package; blend into gelatin. Spoon into 1-quart mold or sherbet glasses. Chill until firm. Unmold. Garnish with more whipped cream, if desired. Makes 4 cups, or 6 to 8 servings.

APRICOT BAVARIAN CREAM

An excellently flavored apricot dessert that's a charming finale to a meal.

1½ cups (8 oz.) dried apricots
1 package (3 oz.) Jell-O Orange-Pineapple, Strawberry-Banana, or Lemon Gelatin
½ cup sugar
1 cup boiling water
1 envelope Dream Whip Whipped Topping Mix or 1 cup whipping cream

Cover apricots with water. Bring to a boil; then cover, reduce heat, and simmer until tender. Drain, reserving liquid. If necessary, add water to make 1 cup. Mash apricots; set aside.

Dissolve Jell-O Gelatin and sugar in boiling water. Add apricot liquid and mashed apricots. Chill until slightly thickened. Prepare whipped topping mix as directed on package or whip the cream; blend into gelatin mixture. Pour into a 1½-quart mold or pile lightly in sherbet glasses. Chill until firm. Unmold. Makes about 5 cups, or 10 servings.

NOTE: If desired, substitute 2 cans (1 lb. each) apricot halves, drained and mashed, for the dried apricots; using ¾ cup drained syrup instead of apricot liquid in recipe and reducing sugar to ¼ cup.

BANANA NUT RING

A lovely finale for any meal — a golden ring of bananas and nuts filled with a fluffy pineapple mixture.

2 packages (3 oz. each) Jell-O Orange-Pineapple or Lemon Gelatin
2 cups boiling water
1 can (13½ oz.) pineapple tidbits
½ cup chopped pecans

2 bananas, sliced
1 envelope Dream Whip Whipped Topping Mix or 1 cup whipping cream
2 tablespoons slivered candied ginger (optional)
Maraschino cherries

Dissolve Jell-O Gelatin in boiling water. Drain pineapple, measuring syrup. Add cold water to make 1½ cups; add to gelatin. Chill until very thick. Fold in pecans and bananas. Pour into a 1½-quart ring mold. Chill until firm. Prepare whipped topping mix as directed on package or whip the cream; fold in drained pineapple and ginger. Chill. To serve, unmold ring and spoon pineapple mixture into center. Garnish with quartered maraschino cherries, if desired. Makes about 5 cups gelatin and 2 cups pineapple mixture, or 8 to 10 servings.

MILK SHERBET

You'll find a delicious, easy-to-make sherbet handy for all occasions.

1 package (3 oz.) Jell-O Orange, Black Cherry, or Black Raspberry Gelatin
Dash of salt
½ cup sugar
1 cup boiling water
2 cups milk*

*Or use 1 cup evaporated milk and 1 cup water.

Dissolve Jell-O Gelatin, salt, and sugar in boiling water. Chill until slightly syrupy. Then gradually add milk, stirring constantly. Pour into an 8-inch square pan or a freezing tray. Freeze quickly until firm about ½ inch around edges—about 1 hour. Then pour into chilled bowl; beat with rotary beater until fluffy. Return to pan; freeze until firm—at least 5 hours. Makes 3 cups, or 6 servings.

Orange-Pineapple Sherbet: Prepare Milk Sherbet, using Jell-O Orange-Pineapple Gelatin and substituting 2 cups pineapple juice for the milk.

Crown Jewel Dessert as a mold, a pie, and a spring-form pan dessert.

CROWN JEWEL DESSERT
(Broken Window Glass Cake)
(Pictured above)

A spectacular dessert that fits busy schedules — the gelatin for cubes may be made one day, remainder of dessert can wait until the next day.

1 package (3 oz.) **each**
   Jell-O Orange, Cherry, and Lime Gelatins
4 cups boiling water
1½ cups cold water
1 package (3 oz.) Jell-O Lemon Gelatin
¼ cup sugar
½ cup pineapple juice
1½ cups graham cracker crumbs*
⅓ cup melted butter or margarine*
2 envelopes Dream Whip Whipped Topping Mix or 2 cups whipping cream

*Or use 16 to 18 ladyfingers, split, to line pan instead of crumb-butter mixture.

Prepare the three flavors of gelatin separately, using 1 cup boiling water and ½ cup cold water for each. Pour each flavor into an 8-inch square pan. Chill until firm, or overnight.

Then combine the lemon gelatin, sugar, and remaining 1 cup boiling water; stir until gelatin and sugar are dissolved. Stir in pineapple juice. Chill until slightly thickened. Meanwhile, mix the crumbs and melted butter; press into bottom of 9-inch spring-form pan. (If desired, press part of crumbs on sides of pan.)

Cut the firm gelatins into ½-inch cubes. Then prepare whipped topping mix as directed on package or whip the cream; blend with lemon gelatin. Fold in gelatin cubes. Pour into pan. Chill at least 5 hours, or overnight. Run knife or spatula between sides of dessert and pan, and remove sides of pan before serving. If desired, spread additional prepared whipped topping or whipped cream on top and sides. Makes 16 servings.

NOTE: Other Jell-O Gelatin fruit flavors may be used instead of those suggested in recipe, forming any combination of colors desired. For instance, make all the cubes of Jell-O Black Raspberry or Lime Gelatin and substitute Jell-O Strawberry Gelatin for the lemon gelatin.

Crown Jewel Pie: (Pictured on opposite page) Prepare Crown Jewel Dessert, pouring mixture into 2 ladyfinger- or crumb-lined 9-inch pie pans. (To line pie pans with ladyfingers, use about 18 ladyfingers, split. Line the bottoms of the pans; then cut remaining ladyfingers in half crosswise and line the sides of the pans.)

Crown Jewel Cheese Dessert: Prepare Crown Jewel Dessert, substituting 2 packages (3 oz. each) cream cheese, beaten with ¼ cup milk until fluffy, for the whipped topping.

Crown Jewel Mold: (Pictured on opposite page) Prepare Crown Jewel Dessert, omitting crumb mixture and pouring mixture into a 3-quart mold or 9-inch spring-form pan.

GINGER FRUIT MOLD

Ginger ale and candied ginger add distinctive flavors to these fruits.

**2 packages (3 oz. each)
Jell-O Lemon or Strawberry
Punch Gelatin
1¼ cups boiling water
1 can (8¾ oz.) pineapple tidbits
1½ cups ginger ale
1 can (11 oz.) mandarin orange
sections, drained
⅓ cup seedless green grapes
2 tablespoons minced
crystallized ginger**

Dissolve Jell-O Gelatin in boiling water. Drain pineapple, reserving ½ cup syrup. Stir reserved syrup and ginger ale into gelatin. Chill until very thick. Fold in pineapple, orange sections, grapes, and minced ginger. Pour into a 1½-quart mold. Chill until firm. Unmold. Makes about 6 cups, or 12 servings.

CHERRY COLA MOLD

Your favorite cola beverage gives distinctive flavor to a gelatin dessert.

**1 package (8 oz.) cream cheese,
softened
¼ cup mayonnaise
1 package (3 oz.) each Jell-O
Cherry and Strawberry Gelatins
1 cup boiling water
1 can (1 lb. 1 oz.) pitted dark
sweet cherries
1 can (13½ oz.) pineapple tidbits
1 bottle (7 oz.) cola beverage
1 cup chopped nuts**

Blend cream cheese and mayonnaise until smooth. Dissolve Jell-O Gelatins in boiling water. Stir into cheese mixture, blending well. Drain cherries and pineapple, measuring 1½ cups syrup. Then add syrup and cola beverage to gelatin. Chill until very thick. Fold in cherries, pineapple, and nuts. Pour into a 1½-quart mold. Chill until firm. Unmold. Makes about 6½ cups, or 12 servings.

MACAROON VELVET

Crumbled macaroons and toasted almonds add crunchy texture.

**1 package (3 oz.) Jell-O Cherry,
Strawberry-Banana, or
Concord Grape Gelatin
2 tablespoons sugar
¼ teaspoon salt
1 cup boiling water
1 cup cold water
1 cup whipped cream or prepared
Dream Whip Whipped Topping
½ teaspoon vanilla
6 large macaroons, crumbled
¼ cup chopped toasted almonds**

Dissolve Jell-O Gelatin, sugar, and salt in boiling water. Add cold water. Chill until slightly thickened. Blend in remaining ingredients. Spoon into individual molds or serving dishes. Chill until firm. Unmold. Garnish with additional whipped cream or prepared whipped topping, if desired. Makes 3⅔ cups, or about 6 servings.

Creamy Freeze—a frozen treat flavored with Jell-O Gelatin.

CREAMY FREEZE
(Pictured above)

Use any luscious fruit flavor gelatin for a creamy, smooth frozen dessert.

> 1 package (3 oz.) Jell-O Gelatin
>   (any fruit flavor)
> ¾ cup sugar
>   Dash of salt
> 1 cup boiling water
> 2 cups milk
> 1 envelope Dream Whip Whipped
>   Topping Mix or 1 cup whipping
>   cream

Dissolve Jell-O Gelatin, sugar, and salt in boiling water. Blend in milk. (Mixture may look curdled, but will become smooth.) Pour into a freezer tray. Freeze 45 minutes, or until mixture is frozen ½ inch around edges of tray. Meanwhile, prepare whipped topping mix as directed on package or whip the cream. Then beat gelatin mixture until light and fluffy, about 5 minutes. Fold in prepared whipped topping or cream. Pour into two freezer trays and freeze 30 minutes. Empty into a chilled bowl; beat until smooth but not melted. Pour into trays. Freeze until firm — at least 3 hours. Makes 5 cups, or 8 servings.

De Luxe Freeze: Prepare Creamy Freeze, decreasing milk to 1⅔ cups;

then blend in ⅓ cup bourbon or wine when adding prepared whipped topping. Good flavor combinations are Jell-O Raspberry Gelatin and bourbon, Jell-O Mixed Fruit Gelatin and Burgundy, and Jell-O Lime or Lemon Gelatin and dry vermouth.

ICE CREAM PARTY DESSERT
An ice cream and gelatin mixture for a special occasion.

> 2 packages (3 oz. each)
>   Jell-O Concord Grape,
>   Black Raspberry, or
>   Raspberry Gelatin
> 3½ cups boiling water
> 1 quart vanilla ice cream
> 12 ladyfingers, split

Dissolve Jell-O Gelatin in boiling water. Add ice cream by spoonfuls and stir until melted. Chill, stirring occasionally until very thick. Trim ladyfingers to about 2½-inch lengths; place around sides of 9-inch springform pan. Stir gelatin mixture and pour into pan. Chill until firm. Before serving, loosen and remove sides of pan. Garnish with sweetened whipped cream or prepared Dream Whip Whipped Topping and fruit, if desired. Makes 12 servings.

PLUM PUDDING
A make-ahead holiday dessert that's simple to prepare.

> 1 package (3 oz.) Jell-O Lemon
>   or Orange Gelatin
>   Dash of salt
> 1 cup boiling water
> ½ teaspoon cinnamon
> ¼ teaspoon cloves
> 1 cup cold water
> ¾ cup finely cut raisins
> ¾ cup finely cut cooked prunes
> ¼ cup finely cut citron
> ¾ cup finely chopped nuts
> ¾ cup Post Grape-Nuts Cereal

Dissolve Jell-O Gelatin and salt in boiling water. Add spices and cold water. Chill until very thick. Fold in fruits, nuts, and cereal. Spoon into a 1-quart mold. Chill until firm. Unmold. Serve with a custard or hard sauce, if desired. Makes about 4 cups, or 8 to 10 servings.

NOTE: If desired, 1¾ cups cooked dried figs may be substituted for the raisins, prunes, and citron, and ¾ cup crushed vanilla wafers or graham crackers for the cereal.

LEMON CRUMB DESSERT

Excellent for a crowd—make half for smaller groups or your family.

**2 packages (3 oz. each) or
1 package (6 oz.) Jell-O
Lemon Gelatin
1½ cups sugar
¼ teaspoon salt
2 cups boiling water
1½ teaspoons grated lemon rind
⅔ cup lemon juice
3⅓ cups (2 tall cans) undiluted
evaporated milk, chilled
⅔ cup melted butter or margarine
4 cups vanilla wafer or graham
cracker crumbs**

Dissolve Jell-O Gelatin, sugar, and salt in boiling water. Add lemon rind and juice. Chill until very thick. Add evaporated milk and whip until fluffy. Meanwhile, mix butter and vanilla wafer crumbs. Press firmly into two 11x7x1½-inch or 9-inch square pans or four 8-inch pie pans, reserving about ⅓ cup for garnish. Spoon gelatin mixture into pans. Sprinkle with reserved crumbs. Chill until firm. Makes 24 servings.

DOUBLE DECKER DESSERT

Pear slices in one layer and sour cream and cranberry sauce in a second layer result in a delicious treat.

**2 packages (3 oz. each) or
1 package (6 oz.) Jell-O Raspberry or Cherry Gelatin
2 cups boiling water
1½ cups cold water
1 cup pear slices**

**1 tablespoon chopped candied
ginger
½ cup sour cream
1 cup whole cranberry sauce**

Dissolve Jell-O Gelatin in boiling water. Combine 1 cup with ½ cup cold water. Pour into a tall 1½-quart mold; chill until set, but not firm. Add 1 cup cold water to remaining gelatin. Chill until slightly thickened. Arrange pear slices on gelatin in mold. Cover with a little thickened gelatin. Sprinkle with ginger. Chill until set, but not firm. Combine remaining gelatin, sour cream, and cranberry sauce. Pour into mold; chill until firm. Unmold. Makes about 5½ cups, or 10 servings.

PINEAPPLE CHEESE DESSERT
(Pictured on page 4)

A creamy, no-bake cheesecake, glazed with pineapple.

**Crumb Crust (page 32)
1 can (8¾ oz.) crushed pineapple
1 package (3 oz.) Jell-O Orange-
Pineapple or Lemon Gelatin
1¼ cups boiling water
1 package (3 oz.) cream cheese,
softened
¼ teaspoon grated orange or
lemon rind
3 tablespoons sugar
½ teaspoon vanilla
1 cup sour cream**

Prepare Crumb Crust in an 8-inch square pan or a 9-inch pie pan. Drain pineapple, reserving syrup. Dissolve Jell-O Gelatin in boiling water. Add syrup; cool slightly. Meanwhile, blend cream cheese, orange rind, sugar, and vanilla. Combine ½ cup gelatin and the pineapple. Gradually blend remaining gelatin into cheese mixture until smooth. Fold in sour cream. Pour into Crumb Crust. Chill until set, but not firm. Then carefully spoon on pineapple. Chill until firm. Makes about 8 or 9 servings.

NOTE: If desired, recipe may be doubled and chilled in 9-inch square pan.

DE LUXE CHERRY DESSERT

A fluffy topping covers a delicious dark sweet cherry mixture.

1 tablespoon cornstarch
1 can (1 lb. 1 oz.) pitted dark
   sweet cherries
¼ cup brandy or 1 teaspoon
   rum extract
1 package (3 oz.) Jell-O Mixed
   Fruit or Cherry Gelatin
1 tablespoon sugar
1 cup boiling water
1 cup cold water
2 tablespoons brandy or 1 teaspoon rum extract
1 cup prepared Dream Whip
   Whipped Topping

Mix cornstarch and about ¼ cup syrup from cherries, stirring until smooth. Add cherries and ¼ cup brandy. Cook and stir over medium heat until thickened and clear. Pour into 8 dessert dishes. Chill 20 minutes. Dissolve Jell-O Gelatin and sugar in boiling water. Add cold water and 2 tablespoons brandy. Chill until slightly thickened. Blend in the prepared topping. Spoon into dishes. Chill until firm. Makes 5 cups, or 8 servings.

SOUR CREAM DESSERT

A refreshing blend of sour cream and your favorite flavor of gelatin.

1 package (3 oz.) Jell-O Gelatin
   (any fruit flavor)
1 tablespoon sugar
⅛ teaspoon salt
1½ cups boiling water
1 cup light cream
½ teaspoon vanilla
½ cup sour cream

Dissolve Jell-O Gelatin, sugar, and salt in boiling water. Stir in light cream and vanilla. (Mixture may look curdled, but will become smooth.) Stir in sour cream. Chill until slightly thickened. Beat until smooth. Pour into 3- or 4-cup ring mold. Chill until firm. Unmold. Serve with fruit, if desired. Makes 3 cups, or 6 servings.

PEACHY BERRY MOLD

A fruit mold that brings a bit of sunshine to your meal anytime of year.

1 package (3 oz.) Jell-O Orange
   or Orange-Pineapple Gelatin
1 cup boiling water
1 can (8¾ oz.) sliced peaches
1 package (10 oz.) Birds Eye
   Red Raspberries

Dissolve Jell-O Gelatin in boiling water. Drain peaches, measuring syrup; add water to make ¾ cup. Stir into gelatin. Add frozen raspberries, separating berries with fork and stirring until mixture thickens. Then stir in peaches. Pour into serving dishes or a 1-quart serving bowl. Chill until firm. Garnish with sour cream, if desired. Makes 3½ cups, or 6 servings.
NOTE: To substitute fresh raspberries, add ½ cup cold water to gelatin and chill until very thick; then stir in 1 cup fresh raspberries and the peaches.

CHERRY BURGUNDY DESSERT

One of the easiest, most elegant desserts you could make—use fresh, frozen, or canned peaches on it.

1 package (3 oz.) Jell-O Cherry
   Gelatin
1 cup boiling water
¾ cup Burgundy wine*
   Dash of cinnamon
1 cup whipped cream or prepared
   Dream Whip Whipped Topping
1 cup sweetened sliced peaches,
   drained

*Or use 1 bottle (7 oz.) ginger ale.

Dissolve Jell-O Gelatin in boiling water. Cool; then add wine. Pour into 1-quart mold or individual molds. Chill until firm. Add cinnamon to whipped cream. Unmold gelatin. Garnish with peaches and whipped cream. Makes 2 cups gelatin, or 4 servings.

Fruited Burgundy Dessert: Prepare Cherry Burgundy Dessert, chilling gelatin until very thick and adding peaches before pouring into molds.

Birthday Surprise—a cool, delightful dessert for summer parties.

BIRTHDAY SURPRISE
(Pictured above)

A shimmering, colorful ring of gelatin filled with ice cream can replace the traditional cake.

> 2 packages (3 oz. each) or
> 1 package (6 oz.) Jell-O Straw-
>   berry-Banana Gelatin*
> 2 cups boiling water
> 1½ cups cold water
> 1 pint <u>each</u> vanilla <u>and</u> straw-
>   berry ice creams
> Marshmallows and gumdrops

*Or use your favorite fruit flavor.

Dissolve Jell-O Gelatin in boiling water. Add cold water. Pour into a 1-quart ring mold; chill until firm. Unmold and fill center of ring with ice creams. Place marshmallows and gumdrops around gelatin, using gumdrops as holders for birthday candles, if desired. Makes 3½ cups gelatin, or about 6 servings.

CHERRY CHARLOTTE RUSSE

Make individual desserts for a party or for hungry homecomers.

> 1 package (3 oz.) Jell-O Black
>   Cherry or Cherry Gelatin
> ¼ cup sugar
> 1 cup boiling water
> ¾ cup cold water
> 1 cup whipping cream or 1 enve-
>   lope Dream Whip Whipped
>   Topping Mix
> ¼ cup chopped pecans
> 16 ladyfingers, split

Dissolve Jell-O Gelatin and sugar in boiling water. Add cold water. Chill until slightly thickened. Whip cream or prepare whipped topping mix as directed on package. Fold nuts and whipped cream into gelatin. Arrange ladyfingers around sides of serving dishes; then pour gelatin mixture into dishes. Chill until firm. Makes about 4 cups, or 8 servings.

Charlotte Russe Imperial—a regal dessert for special occasions.

CHARLOTTE RUSSE IMPERIAL
(Pictured above)

Custard plus fruit gelatin makes a velvety, extra-special dessert.

3 egg yolks, slightly beaten
¼ teaspoon salt
2 cups milk
1 package (3 oz.) Jell-O Gelatin
   (any fruit flavor)
½ cup boiling water
3 egg whites
¼ cup sugar
½ cup whipping cream or 1 envelope Dream Whip Whipped
   Topping Mix
½ teaspoon vanilla
¼ cup chopped pecans (optional)
16 ladyfingers, split

Cook egg yolks, salt, and milk in double boiler until mixture coats metal spoon, stirring constantly. Dissolve Jell-O Gelatin in boiling water. Very slowly stir into milk mixture. Chill until slightly thickened. Beat egg whites until they form soft peaks. Gradually add sugar, beating until stiff peaks form. Whip the cream with the vanilla, or prepare whipped topping mix according to package directions. Fold pecans, egg whites, and whipped cream, or 1 cup prepared whipped topping, into gelatin mixture. Line a 9x5x3-inch loaf pan or 2-quart bowl or mold with ladyfingers. Then add gelatin mixture. Chill until firm.

Unmold. Garnish with the remaining whipped topping, if desired. Makes 5⅔ cups, or 8 servings.

CRANBERRY SQUARES

A light, not too sweet dessert is sure to please after a lavish meal.

2 cups fresh cranberries
½ cup water
¾ cup sugar
1 package (3 oz.) Jell-O Lemon
   or Orange-Pineapple Gelatin
1 cup boiling water
1 envelope Dream Whip Whipped
   Topping Mix or 1 cup whipping cream
Crumb Crust (page 32)
1 tablespoon grated orange rind

Cook cranberries in ½ cup water until skins burst. Add sugar and stir until dissolved. Dissolve Jell-O Gelatin in 1 cup boiling water; add to cranberry mixture. Chill until slightly thickened. Prepare whipped topping mix as directed on package or whip the cream. Blend into cranberry mixture. Prepare Crumb Crust mixture, using vanilla wafer crumbs and adding grated orange rind. Spread ⅔ of crumb mixture on bottom of a greased 8-inch square pan. Pour filling over it; top with remaining crumb mixture. Chill until firm. Makes 9 servings.

Pineapple-Cranberry Squares: Prepare Cranberry Squares, blending 1 can (13½ oz.) drained crushed pineapple into cranberry mixture before adding prepared whipped topping.

FRUIT DESSERT ELEGANT

Captured in luscious whipped gelatin dessert are three fruits, sour cream, marshmallows, and nuts.

1 package (3 oz.) Jell-O Strawberry-Banana or Raspberry
   Gelatin
1 tablespoon sugar
⅛ teaspoon salt
1 cup boiling water

1 package (10 oz.) Birds Eye
  Red Raspberries, thawed
1 can (8¾ oz.) crushed
  pineapple
1 cup sour cream
2 medium bananas, sliced
1 cup miniature marshmallows
½ to 1 cup chopped walnuts

Dissolve Jell-O Gelatin, sugar, and salt in boiling water. Drain raspberries and pineapple, reserving ¾ cup of the combined syrups. Add measured syrups to gelatin. Chill until very thick. Then whip until fluffy—see directions on page 84. Beat sour cream until smooth; fold into gelatin mixture. Then stir in fruits, marshmallows, and walnuts. Chill 15 minutes; then stir and spoon into a 2-quart mold or bowl. Chill until firm. Unmold and spoon into dessert dishes before serving. Makes about 7 cups, or 8 to 10 servings.

NOTE: This delicious dessert is so rich and full of fruit that it has a rather soft set. Therefore, a shallow mold is most satisfactory.

MARBLE-TOP DESSERT

Gelatin marbled with whipped cream is a glamorous topping for fruited gelatin squares.

1 can (1 lb. 4½ oz.) pineapple
  tidbits
1 package (6 oz.) Jell-O Strawberry Gelatin
¼ cup sugar
⅛ teaspoon salt
2 cups boiling water
1 cup cold water
1 cup whipped cream or prepared
  Dream Whip Whipped Topping

Drain pineapple, measuring syrup. Arrange pineapple in a single layer in an 8-inch square pan. Dissolve Jell-O Gelatin, sugar, and salt in boiling water. Add a little cold water to pineapple syrup to make ¾ cup; add to gelatin. Set aside 1 cup gelatin

mixture. Pour remaining gelatin over pineapple in pan. Chill until firm. Meanwhile, add 1 cup cold water to reserved gelatin. Chill until very thick. Then mix with whipped cream just enough to marble. Chill until set. To serve, top squares of the pineapple and gelatin mixture with a spoonful of marbled gelatin. Makes about 6 cups, or 9 servings.

NOTE: If desired, spoon whipped cream mixture over firm gelatin in pan and chill until serving time.

BAKED ALASKA

One of the world's most elegant desserts is easy to make at home with fruit flavor gelatin.

2 packages (3 oz. each) Jell-O
  Gelatin (any fruit flavor)
2 cups boiling water
½ cup chilled ginger ale or
  cold water
1 pint vanilla ice cream,
  slightly softened
3 egg whites
6 tablespoons sugar

Dissolve 1 package Jell-O Gelatin in 1 cup boiling water; stir in ginger ale. Pour into an 8x4x3-inch loaf pan; chill until firm. Dissolve remaining package Jell-O Gelatin in 1 cup boiling water. Spoon in ice cream, stirring until blended. Chill until thickened. Cut firm gelatin into ½-inch cubes. Fold into creamy, thickened gelatin. Spoon into an 8x4x3-inch loaf pan or 1-quart mold or bowl. Chill until firm. Unmold on an oven-proof platter; chill until platter is cold.

Beat egg whites until foamy throughout. Add sugar 2 tablespoons at a time, beating thoroughly after each addition; then beat until stiff, shiny peaks will form. Completely cover loaf with meringue, carefully sealing around base. Bake in hot oven (500° F.) until golden brown, about 2 minutes. Chill until serving time. Makes about 4 cups gelatin, or 8 servings.

RIBBON LOAF

A colorful, exciting "something different" for a bridge party snack.

**1 package (3 oz.) each Jell-O Lime
and Raspberry Gelatins
1½ cups (15-oz. jar) applesauce
18 double graham crackers
1 envelope Dream Whip Whipped
Topping Mix
¼ teaspoon almond extract
3 tablespoons confectioners'
sugar
¼ cup toasted chopped blanched
almonds**

Combine each package of Jell-O Gelatin with ¾ cup applesauce; stir until well blended, about 1½ minutes. Place 2 double crackers end to end on platter. Spread with ¼ cup lime mixture. Top with 2 double crackers; spread with ¼ cup raspberry mixture. Continue layers, alternating flavors and ending with crackers.

Prepare whipped topping mix as directed on package, using ¼ teaspoon almond extract instead of vanilla. Add confectioners' sugar. Spread over sides and top of loaf. Sprinkle sides with almonds. Chill at least 30 minutes. Makes 12 to 14 servings.

COOKY STACKS

Looking for a new treat for your next party? This is sure to be the delight of all the children!

**1 package (3 oz.) Jell-O Strawberry-
Banana or Cherry Gelatin
1 cup boiling water
1 cup cold water
1 cup whipping cream or
1 envelope Dream Whip
Whipped Topping Mix
32 thin chocolate cookies
(2½ inches wide)
8 maraschino cherries**

Dissolve Jell-O Gelatin in boiling water. Add cold water. Chill until very thick. Then whip until fluffy—see directions on page 84. Whip and sweeten the cream or prepare the topping mix as directed on the package. Fold 1 cup into the whipped gelatin. Chill about 10 minutes, or until of spreading consistency. Spread gelatin mixture on 24 of the cookies. Then stack 3 frosted cookies and top with a plain cooky. Continue with remaining cookies, making 8 Cooky Stacks. Place on wax paper-lined tray or pan. Chill until firm. Top with remaining whipped cream and cherries. Makes 8 servings.

CHERRY CHEESE CHARMER

Want to charm someone special? A dessert of dark cherries, gelatin, and cream cheese should do the trick.

**1 package (3 oz.) Jell-O Cherry
or Black Cherry Gelatin
2 tablespoons sugar
Dash of salt
1 cup boiling water
1 can (8¾ oz.) pitted dark sweet
cherries
1 tablespoon lemon juice
1 package (3 oz.) cream cheese,
softened**

Dissolve Jell-O Gelatin, sugar, and salt in boiling water. Drain cherries, measuring syrup; add water to make ¾ cup, if necessary. Add syrup and lemon juice to gelatin. Gradually blend gelatin into the softened cream cheese. Chill until very thick; then whip until fluffy—see directions on page 84. Fold in drained cherries. Pour into 1-quart mold or an 8x4x3-inch loaf pan. Chill until firm. Unmold and serve with whipped cream or prepared Dream Whip Whipped Topping, if desired. Makes about 3 cups, or 6 servings.

NOTE: If desired, this dessert may be molded in layers. Pour ¾ cup of the gelatin into mold or pan before blending gelatin into cheese. This recipe may be doubled and chilled in a 1½-quart mold or 9x5x3-inch loaf pan to make about 6 cups, or 12 servings.

Upside-Down Cake—peaches glisten in this cool version of a favorite

UPSIDE-DOWN CAKE
(Pictured above)

Using baked cake layers, here's a delicious version of an old favorite.

- 1 package (3 oz.) Jell-O Lemon, Raspberry, Strawberry, or Orange-Pineapple Gelatin
- 1 cup boiling water
- 1 can (1 lb. 1 oz.) sliced peaches or fruit cocktail
- 1 baked 8-inch white cake layer
- Sweetened whipped cream or prepared Dream Whip Whipped Topping

Dissolve Jell-O Gelatin in boiling water. Drain peaches, measuring syrup. Add water to make 1 cup. Add to gelatin. Chill until slightly thickened. Place peaches in an 8-inch layer pan; cover with about 1¼ cups gelatin. Place cake layer on gelatin, top side up. Spread remaining gelatin over cake. Chill until firm. Unmold. Garnish with whipped cream or prepared whipped topping. Makes 6 servings.

APPLE FLUFF

Anyone that likes applesauce will enjoy it molded in fruit flavor gelatin and deliciously spiced.

- 1 package (3 oz.) Jell-O Orange, Lime, Raspberry, or Lemon Gelatin
- 1 cup boiling water
- ⅔ cup cold water
- 1½ cups (15-oz. jar) applesauce
- 1 teaspoon grated lemon rind
- ¼ teaspoon cinnamon
- ⅛ teaspoon ground cloves

Dissolve Jell-O Gelatin in boiling water. Add cold water. Chill until very thick. Then whip until fluffy—see directions on page 84. Fold in applesauce, lemon rind, and spices. Spoon into individual molds or an 8-inch square pan. Chill until firm. Unmold or cut in squares. If desired, serve with custard sauce, sweetened whipped cream, or prepared Dream Whip Whipped Topping. Makes about 5 cups, or 6 to 8 servings.

21

Supreme Dessert—so called because everyone agrees it's truly supreme.

SUPREME DESSERT
(Pictured above)

An elegant dessert to serve in your best stemware on special occasions.

**2 packages (3 oz. each) or
1 package (6 oz.) Jell-O
Gelatin (see Note)
¼ teaspoon salt
2 cups boiling water
1½ cups cold water
1 package (10 oz. to 1 lb.) Birds
Eye Fruit (see Note)
1 cup sour cream, softened
vanilla ice cream, whipped
cream, prepared Dream Whip
Whipped Topping, or vanilla
yogurt
1½ tablespoons brandy***
1½ tablespoons rum*
**2 tablespoons Cointreau or
Curacao***

*Or substitute ½ teaspoon each brandy and rum extracts and 1 teaspoon orange extract.

Dissolve Jell-O Gelatin and salt in boiling water. Add cold water. Measure 2 cups into bowl; add frozen fruit.

Stir, carefully separating fruit with a fork. Chill until mixture is almost set —about 15 minutes. Spoon into sherbet glasses, filling each two-thirds full. Chill until set, but not firm.

Chill remaining gelatin just until slightly thickened. Add remaining ingredients. Beat 1 minute, or until bubbly. Spoon into the glasses. Chill until firm. Makes 6¾ cups, or 6 to 8 servings.

NOTE: Suggested Jell-O Gelatin flavor and frozen fruit combinations are:

Strawberry or mixed fruit gelatin with strawberries

Lemon or strawberry-banana gelatin with mixed fruit

Lime or mixed fruit gelatin with melon balls

Orange-pineapple gelatin with peaches

Raspberry or orange gelatin with red raspberries

Black raspberry gelatin with blueberries

Cherry gelatin with sweet cherries

RING-AROUND-THE-FRUIT
(Pictured on page 4)

A bright, clear gelatin ring frames a whipped cream and fruit mixture.

**2 packages (3 oz. each) or
1 package (6 oz.) Jell-O Strawberry, Raspberry, or Lime Gelatin
2 cups boiling water
1 can (1 lb. 14 oz.) fruit cocktail***
**½ cup maraschino cherry halves
⅓ cup coarsely chopped nuts
½ cup miniature marshmallows
1 cup sweetened whipped cream or prepared Dream Whip Whipped Topping**

*Or use 1 can (1 lb. 1 oz.) fruit cocktail and 1 can (8¾ oz.) pineapple tidbits.

Dissolve Jell-O Gelatin in boiling water. Drain fruit cocktail, measuring syrup. Add water to make 1½ cups. Add to gelatin. Pour into a 1-quart or individual ring molds. Chill until firm. Combine fruit, nuts, and marshmallows. Fold in the whipped cream. Chill. Then unmold gelatin onto large serving plate or platter. Spoon the fruit mixture into center of ring. Makes about 4 cups gelatin and 4 cups fruit mixture, or 8 servings.

Riced Nest Dessert: Prepare Ring-Around-the-Fruit, chilling gelatin in a 9-inch square pan. Then flake gelatin with a fork and arrange like a nest on large plate; spoon fruit into nest.

FRUIT-FILLED ANGEL CAKE

Cake, fruit, and cream are combined in this make-ahead dessert.

**1 baked 10-inch angel food cake
1 package (3 oz.) Jell-O Strawberry, Cherry, or Mixed Fruit Gelatin
1 cup boiling water
⅔ cup cold water or fruit juice
1 cup fresh or drained canned or frozen fruit***
2 cups whipping cream or 2 envelopes Dream Whip Whipped Topping Mix

*Use strawberries, raspberries, cherries, or other fruit. A 10-oz. package of frozen fruit or a 1-lb. can of fruit will be sufficient.

Cut a ½-inch horizontal slice from top of cake. Then carefully hollow out remainder of cake, leaving a ½-inch shell on bottom and sides. Dissolve Jell-O Gelatin in boiling water. Add cold water and fruit. (If canned or frozen fruit is used, substitute the drained fruit syrup for the cold water.) Chill until slightly thickened. Whip the cream or prepare whipped topping mix as directed on package; blend 2 cups into gelatin. Spoon part of the gelatin mixture into hollow in cake. Cut cake from hollow into small pieces; place several pieces on gelatin. Layer gelatin and cake until hollow is filled. Replace top slice. Spread the remaining cream or prepared whipped topping on top and sides of cake. Chill at least 3 hours. Store in refrigerator. Makes 10 to 16 servings.

ORANGE-MALLOW RING

For year 'round refreshment, mold fresh or canned oranges in gelatin.

**1 package (3 oz.) Jell-O Orange or Orange-Pineapple Gelatin
1 cup boiling water
¾ cup cold ginger ale or water
1 cup miniature or quartered marshmallows
1 cup diced fresh orange sections, drained***

*Or use 1 can (11 oz.) mandarin orange sections, drained.

Dissolve Jell-O Gelatin in boiling water. Add ginger ale. Chill until very thick. Stir in marshmallows and orange sections. Pour into a 1-quart ring mold or individual ring molds. Chill until firm. Unmold. Makes 3 cups, or 6 servings.

Strawberry-Banana Ring: Prepare Orange-Mallow Ring, substituting Jell-O Strawberry Punch Gelatin for the orange gelatin and 1 medium banana, sliced, for the oranges.

PINK PARTY DESSERT

No one will suspect you're using leftover angel cake for a party.

2 packages (10 oz. each) Birds Eye Strawberries, thawed
1 package (3 oz.) Jell-O Strawberry Gelatin
½ cup sugar
1 cup boiling water
Angel food cake*

*Use leftover cake (about half of a 9- or 10-inch tube cake) or a commercial angel cake.

Drain thawed berries, reserving ¾ cup syrup. Dissolve Jell-O Gelatin and sugar in boiling water. Add syrup. Chill until very thick. Meanwhile, cut the cake into 1-inch cubes. Arrange half of the cake pieces in a 12x7½x2- or 13x9x2-inch pan. Fold drained berries into gelatin. Pour about half of the mixture over cake. Top with remaining cake and gelatin mixture. Chill until firm. Cut into squares. Makes 12 to 15 servings.

RAINBOW CAKE
(Pictured on page 4)

Five flavors of whipped gelatin form this colorful, spectacular dessert.

1 package (3 oz.) each Jell-O Black Raspberry, Lime, Lemon, Orange, and Strawberry Gelatins
5 cups boiling water
1¼ cups cold water
1 envelope Dream Whip Whipped Topping Mix or 1 cup whipping cream (optional)

Dissolve each package of Jell-O Gelatin separately in 1 cup boiling water. Add ¼ cup cold water to each. Chill black raspberry gelatin until very thick. Smoothly line sides of a 9- or 10-inch spring-form pan with wax paper, cut to extend 3 inches above pan. Whip black raspberry gelatin until fluffy—see directions on page 84. Spoon into pan. Chill until set, but not firm. Chill, whip, and layer remaining flavors in pan, letting each layer chill until set, but not firm before adding next layer. Chill until firm or overnight. Loosen around edges and remove sides of pan and paper. Prepare whipped topping mix as directed on package or whip cream; spread over top and sides of cake. Makes about 14 cups, or 12 servings.

Rainbow Dessert: Prepare Rainbow Cake using only 3 gelatin flavors (1 package each Jell-O Raspberry, Lemon, and Lime Gelatins), 3 cups boiling water, and ¾ cup cold water; mold dessert in a 9-inch spring-form pan or 10-inch tube pan.

STRAWBERRY WHIP

Three kinds of "strawberry" blended in one delicious, fluffy dessert.

1 package (3 oz.) Jell-O Strawberry Gelatin
3 tablespoons sugar
1½ cups boiling water
1 package (10 oz.) Birds Eye Strawberries
1 package Jell-O Whip 'n Chill Strawberry Dessert Mix
½ cup cold milk
½ cup cold water

Dissolve Jell-O Gelatin and sugar in boiling water. Add strawberries; stir until berries thaw and separate. Chill until very thick. Prepare dessert mix with milk and cold water as directed on package; add to gelatin. Beat at medium speed of electric mixer for 1 minute. If necessary, chill until mixture mounds—about 10 minutes. Then stir and spoon into 1½-quart mold. Chill until firm. Unmold. Makes about 5½ cups, or 7 or 8 servings.

FRUIT PUDDING

Unusual gelatin dessert containing raisins, dates, figs, banana, and nuts.

1 package (3 oz.) Jell-O Cherry or Mixed Fruit Gelatin
¼ teaspoon salt
1 cup boiling water

1 cup cold water
½ cup chopped seedless raisins
½ cup finely cut dates
⅔ cup finely cut dried figs
1 banana, diced
¼ cup chopped nuts

Dissolve Jell-O Gelatin and salt in boiling water. Add cold water. Chill until very thick. Then fold in fruits and nuts. Pour into a 1-quart mold. Chill until firm. Unmold. If desired, serve with custard sauce. Makes about 4 cups, or 8 servings.

JEWELLED DESSERT

The fruits studding the creamy gelatin of this dessert sparkle like precious jewels.

  1 package (3 oz.) Jell-O Orange-
     Pineapple or Orange Gelatin
  1 tablespoon sugar
⅛ teaspoon salt
  1 cup boiling water
  1 can (11 oz.) mandarin oranges*
  1 can (8¾ oz.) pineapple tidbits
  1 cup sour cream or yoghurt
  1 cup Baker's Angel Flake Coconut
  1 cup miniature marshmallows
  1 cup seedless grapes

*Or use 1 cup diced fresh orange sections.

Dissolve Jell-O Gelatin, sugar, and salt in boiling water. Drain oranges and pineapple, measuring combined syrups. Add water to make 1 cup, if necessary; add to gelatin mixture. Stir in sour cream. Chill until very thick. Stir in drained fruits, coconut, marshmallows, and grapes. Chill 15 minutes; then spoon into a 1½-quart mold. Chill until firm. Unmold. Garnish with additional coconut and several seedless grapes or maraschino cherry halves, if desired. Makes 5½ cups, or 8 to 10 servings.

Multi-Jewel Dessert: Prepare Jewelled Dessert, substituting 1 can (1 lb. 1 oz.) fruit cocktail for the pineapple tidbits and grapes. If desired, 1 cup diced large marshmallows may be used instead of the miniature marshmallows.

CHERRY-MALLOW MEDLEY

Dark sweet cherries and marshmallows dot a fluffy gelatin mixture.

  1 can (1 lb. 1 oz.) pitted dark
     sweet cherries
1½ cups miniature or diced
     marshmallows
  1 package (3 oz.) Jell-O Black
     Cherry or Cherry Gelatin
  1 cup boiling water
½ teaspoon almond extract

Drain cherries, reserving syrup. Mix cherries, marshmallows, and ½ cup of the syrup. Set aside. Dissolve Jell-O Gelatin in boiling water. Add almond extract and remaining cherry syrup. Chill until very thick. Whip until fluffy—see directions on page 84. Fold in cherry mixture. Pour into a 2-quart bowl. Chill until firm. Serve with prepared Dream Whip Whipped Topping, if desired. Makes about 5 cups, or 8 to 10 servings.

Cherry Medley: (Pictured below) Prepare Cherry-Mallow Medley, omitting marshmallows and the whipping of the gelatin. Serve with cream cheese balls, if desired. Makes 3 cups, or 6 servings.

Cherry Medley—dark sweet beauties molded in cherry gelatin.

PEACH AND BANANA MOLD

Fruit flavor gelatin turns a small can of peaches and a single banana into a refreshing dessert for six persons.

> 1 package (3 oz.) Jell-O Lime,
> Lemon, or Orange-
> Pineapple Gelatin
> 1 cup boiling water
> 1 can (8¾ oz.) sliced peaches
> 1 banana, sliced

Dissolve Jell-O Gelatin in boiling water. Drain peaches, measuring syrup. Add water to make 1 cup; add syrup to gelatin. Chill until very thick. Fold in peaches and banana. Pour into a 1-quart mold or serving bowl or into individual molds or dishes. Chill until firm. Unmold. If desired, garnish with additional banana slices rolled in finely chopped nuts. Makes 3 cups, or about 6 servings.

NOTE: If desired, pour 1 cup of the gelatin into mold, chill until slightly thickened, and arrange peaches in gelatin; chill until set, but not firm. Meanwhile, chill remaining gelatin until slightly thickened; pour into mold and insert banana slices around sides. Chill until firm.

GLAZED TEA CAKES

Cake squares glazed with gelatin stay fresh and lovely until served.

> 1 package yellow cake mix
> 1 package (3 oz.) Jell-O Straw-
> berry, Cherry, or Lime Gelatin
> 1 cup boiling water
> 1 cup cold water
> 2 cups finely chopped pecans or
> walnuts

Prepare cake mix according to package directions; bake in 15½ x 10½ x 1-inch pan lined with wax paper. Cool cake; then trim edges and brush off crumbs. Cut into 2-inch squares. Dissolve Jell-O Gelatin in boiling water; add cold water. Chill until syrupy. Dip each cake square in gelatin, coating all sides. Then roll in nuts. Chill until firm. Makes 35 squares.

FRUIT FRAPPES

Reminiscent of old-fashioned ice cream parlor creations.

> 1 package (3 oz.) Jell-O
> Gelatin (any fruit flavor)
> 1 cup boiling water
> 1¼ cups cold water
> 1 pint ice cream (any flavor)
> ½ cup fruit sundae sauce
> 1 cup prepared Dream Whip
> Whipped Topping or
> whipped cream
> ¼ cup chopped nuts
> 4 stemmed maraschino cherries

Dissolve Jell-O Gelatin in boiling water; add cold water. Chill until set, but not firm. Alternately spoon layers of ice cream and gelatin into 4 tall sundae glasses, ending with gelatin and leaving about ½-inch space. Top gelatin with sundae sauce, prepared whipped topping, nuts, and cherries. Insert slim cream-filled wafers in each, if desired. Makes 4 servings.

PINK COCONUT CAKE

Gelatin adds flavor and color to both the cake and its coconut garnish.

> 1 package (3 oz.) Jell-O Gelatin
> (any red fruit flavor)
> 1⅓ cups (about) Baker's Angel
> Flake Coconut
> 1 package white cake mix
> 2 egg whites
> Water
> Fluffy white frosting

Combine 1 tablespoon Jell-O Gelatin and the coconut in a jar, cover, and shake until coconut is tinted. Prepare cake mix with egg whites and water as directed on package, adding remaining Jell-O Gelatin before beating. (Some undissolved gelatin may remain after beating.) Pour into 2 round 9-inch layer pans that are greased, floured, and lined with wax paper. Bake in moderate oven (350°F.) until cakes pull away from sides of pans and test done in centers. Cool in pans 10 minutes; then remove from pans and cool on racks. Split layers horizontally, making 4 layers. Fill and frost with a fluffy white frosting; sprinkle with tinted coconut.

FRUIT-FILLED CAKE ROLL
(Pictured below)
Gelatin and frozen raspberries—a delicious filling for a cake roll.

¾ cup sifted Swans Down Cake
   Flour
¾ teaspoon Calumet Baking
   Powder
¼ teaspoon salt
4 eggs (at room temperature)
¾ cup sugar
1 teaspoon vanilla
1⅓ cups (about) Baker's Angel
   Flake Coconut
1 package (3 oz.) Jell-O Raspberry Gelatin*
1 cup boiling water
1 package (10 oz.) Birds Eye
   Red Raspberries*

*Or use Jell-O Strawberry-Banana Gelatin and Birds Eye Strawberries.

Sift flour, baking powder, and salt together. Beat eggs. Gradually add sugar, beating until thick and light-colored. Gradually fold in flour mixture; then add vanilla. Pour batter into a 15½x10½x1-inch pan that is greased, lined with wax paper, and greased again. Sprinkle coconut over batter. Bake in a hot oven (400°F.) about 13 minutes. Then turn cake out on cloth that has been sprinkled generously with confectioners' sugar. Remove paper and trim off edges. Roll cake, rolling cloth up with cake. Cool thoroughly on cake rack.

Meanwhile, dissolve Jell-O Gelatin in boiling water. Add frozen fruit and stir until berries separate. Let stand until thickened, stirring occasionally. Then unroll cake, spread with filling, and roll up again. Sprinkle with confectioners' sugar or spread with whipped cream or prepared Dream Whip Whipped Topping, if desired. Chill and store in refrigerator. Makes 10 to 12 servings.

Fruit-Filled Cake Roll—fruited gelatin fills this delicate cake roll.

PINEAPPLE SNOW

A refreshingly light dessert that's easy to prepare for a crowd.

1 package (3 oz.) Jell-O Orange-Pineapple Gelatin
⅛ teaspoon salt
1 cup boiling water
1 cup canned pineapple juice*
1 egg white

*For a firmer snow, use only ¾ cup juice.

Dissolve Jell-O Gelatin and salt in boiling water. Add pineapple juice. Chill until very thick. Then add egg white and whip until fluffy—see directions on page 84. Pile lightly in sherbet glasses or pour into an 8-inch square pan. Chill until firm. If chilled in pan, cut in squares or spoon into dessert dishes. Serve with custard sauce, if desired. Makes about 5 cups, or 6 servings.

Lemon Snow: Prepare Pineapple Snow, using Jell-O Lemon Gelatin instead of orange-pineapple gelatin and substituting ¾ cup cold water and ¼ cup lemon juice for the pineapple juice. Add ½ teaspoon grated lemon rind and 2 tablespoons sugar.

Orange Snow: Prepare Pineapple Snow, using Jell-O Orange or Orange-Pineapple Gelatin and substituting ¾ cup orange juice for pineapple juice. Add ½ teaspoon grated orange rind.

CHRISTMAS FRUIT MOLD

A de luxe mold of fruit and nuts, decorative enough for a holiday table.

2 packages (3 oz. each) or 1 package (6 oz.) Jell-O Lemon or Orange Gelatin
2 cups boiling water
1½ cups cherry kijafa wine*
Blanched almonds, halved
¼ teaspoon cloves
¼ teaspoon cinnamon
⅛ teaspoon allspice
1 cup chopped candied mixed fruit
½ cup light raisins
½ cup currants
½ cup maraschino cherries, halved
½ cup coarsely chopped walnuts

*Or use 1 bottle (12 oz.) ginger ale and 1 teaspoon rum extract.

Dissolve Jell-O Gelatin in boiling water. Add wine. Pour ½ cup into a 1½-quart mold. Chill until set, but not firm. Arrange almonds in decorative pattern on top of set gelatin. Pour ½ cup gelatin over almonds. Chill again until set, but not firm. Meanwhile, add spices, fruit, and walnuts to remaining gelatin; chill until slightly thickened. Then spoon gently over gelatin in mold. Chill until firm. Unmold. Makes 6 cups, or 10 to 12 servings.

BANANA SPLITS

Mounds of gelatin give a soda fountain treat a delicious, new twist.

1 package (3 oz.) each Jell-O Strawberry and Lime Gelatins
2 cups boiling water
2 cups cold water
6 bananas, halved lengthwise
1 pint ice cream
1 can (8¾ oz.) fruit cocktail
½ cup marshmallow sundae sauce
Prepared Dream Whip Whipped Topping or whipped cream
¼ cup chopped nuts

Prepare each flavor of Jell-O Gelatin separately with 1 cup boiling water and 1 cup cold water. Chill until firm. Arrange bananas in 6 shallow dessert dishes; scoop ice cream into center. Spoon strawberry gelatin on one side, lime gelatin on other. Drain fruit; spoon over gelatin. Spoon marshmallow sauce over ice cream. Top with prepared topping, nuts, and maraschino cherries, if desired. Makes 6 splits.

QUICK CHEESE MOLDS

Ice replaces cold water in a speedy blender treat.

1 package (3 oz.) Jell-O Lemon or Lime Gelatin

Fruit Pie Unlimited—one of the possibilities, peaches in orange gelatin.

¾ cup scalded milk
1 package (8 oz.) cream cheese,
    cut in chunks
2 egg yolks
½ cup whipping cream
½ cup crushed ice

Put Jell-O Gelatin and milk into an electric blender; cover and blend 20 seconds. Add cream cheese and egg yolks; blend about 15 seconds. Add cream and ice; just turn blender on and off quickly. Pour into individual molds. Chill until firm—about 45 minutes. Unmold and garnish with Baker's Angel Flake Coconut, if desired. Makes 3 cups, or 6 servings.

FRUIT PIE UNLIMITED
(Pictured above and on page 31)

Your favorite gelatin flavors and fruits can dictate the ingredients.

1 package (3 oz.) Jell-O Gelatin
    (any fruit flavor)
2 to 4 tablespoons sugar (optional)

1 cup boiling water
1 cup cold water
1½ cups fruit*
1 baked 8-inch pastry shell,
    Crumb Crust (page 32), or 6
    to 8 tart shells, cooled

*Use fresh or drained canned or frozen strawberry halves, sliced peaches, red raspberries, sliced bananas, fruit cocktail, or mixed fruit.

Dissolve Jell-O Gelatin and sugar in boiling water. Stir in cold water. Chill until very thick. Then fold in fruit. Pour into pastry shell. Chill until firm. Garnish with whipped cream, prepared Dream Whip Whipped Topping, or sour cream and additional fruit or sprinkle of nutmeg, if desired.

Speedy Fruit Pie: Prepare Fruit Pie Unlimited, using 7 to 10 ice cubes instead of cold water; stir in ice until gelatin thickens—about 3 minutes. Remove unmelted ice and let stand 5 or 6 minutes; then fold in fruit.

29

SAUCY BAVARIAN PIE

A fluffy pie with a delicious sauce, both made from the gelatin mixture.

- 2 packages (3 oz. each) or
  1 package (6 oz.) Jell-O Raspberry Gelatin
- 2 cups boiling water
- 1½ cups cold water
- 1 package (10 oz.) Birds Eye Red Raspberries
- 1 cup whipping cream or 1 envelope Dream Whip Whipped Topping Mix
- 9-inch Crumb Crust (page 32)

Dissolve Jell-O Gelatin in boiling water. Add 1 cup cold water. Then measure 1 cup gelatin and add frozen raspberries and ½ cup cold water, stirring until berries separate. Chill for use as sauce. Chill remaining gelatin until very thick. Then whip until fluffy—see directions on page 84. Whip cream or prepare whipped topping mix as directed on package; fold into whipped gelatin. Spoon into Crumb Crust. Chill until firm. Serve with the raspberry sauce.

NOTE: If desired, instead of raspberry gelatin and raspberries, use Jell-O Strawberry-Banana Gelatin and 1 package (10 oz.) Birds Eye Strawberries, or Jell-O Lemon, Lime, Mixed Fruit, or Orange-Pineapple Gelatin and 1 package (10 oz.) Birds Eye Mixed Fruit.

NESSELRODE BAVARIAN PIE

Rum flavoring plus candied fruits and almonds equal delicious eating.

- 1 package (3 oz.) Jell-O Orange-Pineapple, Orange, or Lemon Gelatin
- ¼ cup sugar
- 1 cup boiling water
- ¾ cup cold water
- 1 envelope Dream Whip Whipped Topping Mix or 1 cup whipping cream
- 1 jar (4 oz.) diced candied fruits

- ⅓ cup chopped toasted almonds
- 1 teaspoon rum extract
- 1 baked 9-inch pie shell, cooled

Dissolve Jell-O Gelatin and sugar in boiling water; add cold water. Chill until slightly thickened. Prepare the topping mix as directed on package or whip the cream; stir 1½ cups into gelatin. Stir in fruits, almonds, and extract. Pour into pie shell. Chill until firm. Before serving, garnish with remaining whipped topping.

NOTE: If desired, Nesselrode Bavarian may be poured into a 1-quart mold or bowl or 6 to 8 serving dishes instead of pie shell.

FRUIT-GLAZED CHEESE PIE

An easy-to-make, creamy cheese pie is delicious with a fruit glaze.

- 1 cup milk
- 4 packages (3 oz. each) cream cheese, softened
- 1 teaspoon vanilla
- 4 tablespoons sugar
- 1 package Jell-O Lemon Instant Pudding
- 1 baked 9-inch pastry shell, cooled
- 1 package (3 oz.) Jell-O Orange-Pineapple, Mixed Fruit, or Strawberry Gelatin
- Dash of salt
- 1 cup boiling water
- ¼ cup cold water
- 1 package (10 oz.) Birds Eye Mixed Fruit

Blend milk into cream cheese. Add vanilla and 2 tablespoons sugar; beat thoroughly. Add Jell-O Instant Pudding. Beat 1 minute. (Do not overbeat.) Pour into pastry shell. Chill until firm. Meanwhile, dissolve Jell-O Gelatin, 2 tablespoons sugar, and the salt in boiling water. Add cold water and frozen fruit, stirring until fruit thaws and separates. Spoon into pie. Chill until firm. Garnish with prepared Dream Whip Whipped Topping or whipped cream, if desired.

Grasshopper Pie, Fruit Pie Unlimited (page 29), and Frosty Pie (page 33).

GRASSHOPPER PIE
(Pictured above)

A gourmet's delight that can be a busy homemaker's specialty.

2 packages (3 oz. each) or
   1 package (6 oz.) Jell-O
   Lime Gelatin
4 tablespoons sugar*
⅛ teaspoon salt
2 cups boiling water
¾ cup cold water*
⅓ cup green crème de menthe*
⅓ cup crème de cacao*
1 teaspoon vanilla
1 egg white
1 envelope Dream Whip Whipped
   Topping Mix or 1 cup
   whipping cream
9- or 10-inch chocolate crumb
   crust (Crumb Crust, page 32)

*To substitute extracts for the liqueurs, increase the sugar to 6 tablespoons and dissolve 4 tablespoons of it with the gelatin, increase cold water to 1 cup, and use 1 teaspoon each mint and brandy extracts instead of liqueurs.

Dissolve Jell-O Gelatin, 2 tablespoons sugar, and the salt in boiling water. Add cold water, liqueurs, and vanilla. Chill until slightly thickened. Beat egg white until foamy. Gradually add remaining sugar, beating after each addition until blended. Then beat until meringue will stand in shiny, soft peaks. Prepare whipped topping mix as directed on package, omitting vanilla, or whip the cream.

Then measure ½ cup gelatin and set aside. Blend meringue and prepared topping into remaining gelatin mixture. Chill until quite thick. Spoon into crust, using as much as possible. (Any remaining filling may be chilled in sherbet glasses for another meal.) Drizzle the reserved clear gelatin over the top of pie; pull spoon through a zigzag course to marble. Chill until firm. Garnish with chocolate curls, if desired.

31

KEY LIME PIE
(Pictured below)

A luscious, delightful pie that was created in the Florida Keys, where limes grow big and juicy.

> 1 package (3 oz.) Jell-O Lime
>   Gelatin
> 1 cup boiling water
> 1 or 2 teaspoons grated lime rind
> ½ cup lime juice
> 1 egg yolk
> 1⅓ cups (15-oz. can) sweetened
>   condensed milk
> 1 teaspoon aromatic bitters
> 1 egg white
>   Few drops green food coloring
>   (optional)
> 1 baked 9-inch pastry shell,
>   cooled*

*Or line pie pan with ladyfingers.

Dissolve Jell-O Gelatin in boiling water. Add lime rind and juice. Beat egg yolk slightly; slowly add gelatin, stirring constantly. Add milk and bitters, stirring until blended. Chill until slightly thickened. Beat egg white until stiff peaks will form; then fold into gelatin mixture. Add food coloring. Pour into pastry shell. Chill until firm. Garnish with whipped cream or prepared Dream Whip Whipped Topping and lime slices, if desired.

CRUMB CRUST

A versatile crust for pies — use your favorite cookies for the crumbs.

> 1¼ cups fine crumbs*
> ¼ cup sugar*
> ¼ cup softened butter or
>   margarine

*Use graham crackers, zweiback, chocolate wafers, or gingersnaps. Or use vanilla wafers or shortbread and reduce sugar to 4 teaspoons.

Combine ingredients and mix well. Press firmly over bottom and sides of a 9-inch pie pan or bottom of 8-inch square pan. Chill for 1 hour, or bake in moderate oven (375°F.) 8 minutes and cool before filling. Fill with ice cream, chiffon, or cream fillings.

For 8-inch Crumb Crust: Reduce crumbs to 1 cup and sugar to 3 tablespoons. Press into an 8-inch pie pan.

For 10-inch Crumb Crust: Increase crumbs to 1½ cups and sugar to ⅓ cup. Press into a 10-inch pie pan.

Key Lime Pie—one of the coolest, most flavorful pies ever made.

APRICOT PIE GLACÉ

A clear layer of sliced apricots tops a creamy apricot-flavored layer.

1 can (8¾ oz.) apricot halves
1 can (12 oz.) apricot nectar
1 package (3 oz.) Jell-O Orange Gelatin
4 teaspoons lemon juice
¼ teaspoon almond extract
1 envelope Dream Whip Whipped Topping Mix or 1 cup whipping cream
1 baked 9-inch pastry shell, cooled

Drain apricots, reserving syrup. Slice apricots. Add apricot syrup to nectar to make 2 cups. Bring 1 cup nectar to a boil. Dissolve Jell-O Gelatin in boiling nectar. Add remaining 1 cup nectar, the lemon juice, and almond extract. Chill until slightly thickened. Prepare whipped topping mix as directed on package or whip the cream; blend 1 cup into 1 cup of the gelatin. Spoon into pastry shell. Chill until set, but not firm.

Meanwhile, chill remaining gelatin until very thick. Fold in sliced apricots. Spoon onto pie. Chill until firm. Garnish with remaining whipped topping or whipped cream.

FROSTY STRAWBERRY PIE

One of the most popular pies ever created—a delightful blend of fruit flavor gelatin, ice cream, and fruit.

1 package (10 oz.) Birds Eye Strawberries, thawed
1 package (3 oz.) Jell-O Strawberry or Mixed Fruit Gelatin
1 pint vanilla or strawberry ice cream
1 baked 9-inch pastry shell, cooled

Drain strawberries, measuring syrup. Add water to syrup to make 1 cup. Bring liquid to a boil; then add gelatin and stir until dissolved. Spoon in ice cream, stirring until melted and smooth. Chill until thickened, about 20 minutes. Fold in strawberries. Pour into pastry shell. Chill until firm, about 1½ hours or longer. Garnish with prepared Dream Whip Whipped Topping or whipped cream, if desired.

NOTE: About ¾ to 1 cup sliced fresh strawberries may be substituted for the frozen berries, using 1 cup boiling water instead of the syrup mixture and dissolving ¼ cup sugar in the water with the gelatin.

For Other Frosty Pies: Use other flavors of Jell-O Gelatin and other fruits. If desired, syrup drained from frozen or canned fruit may be substituted for all or part of the 1 cup liquid. Other flavors of ice cream may be used, but do not use sherbets or ices.

Frosty Meringue Pie: Prepare any Frosty Pie; chill until firm. Then beat 2 egg whites until foamy; gradually add ¼ cup sugar. Continue beating until stiff peaks form. Spread on pie, sealing well around edges. Place under preheated broiler only until lightly browned—about 3 minutes.

CHERRY PIE

An easy-to-make version of the all-time favorite fruit pie.

1 package (3 oz.) Jell-O Black Cherry or Cherry Gelatin
⅛ teaspoon cinnamon
¾ cup sugar
1 cup boiling water
1 can (1 lb.) pitted red sour cherries
½ cup chopped nuts
1 baked 9-inch pastry shell, cooled

Dissolve Jell-O Gelatin, cinnamon, and sugar in boiling water. Drain cherries, measuring ½ cup of the syrup; stir into gelatin. Chill until very thick. Then add cherries and nuts. Pour into pastry shell. Chill until firm. Garnish with prepared Dream Whip Whipped Topping or whipped cream, if desired.

RASPBERRY GLACÉ PIE

Beautiful fruit shines in a clear, flavorful gelatin glaze, on creamy filling.

1 package (3 oz.) Jell-O Raspberry or Black Raspberry Gelatin
½ cup sugar*
¼ teaspoon salt
1½ cups boiling water
2 tablespoons lemon juice
1⅓ cups whipped cream or prepared Dream Whip Whipped Topping
1 baked 9-inch pastry shell, cooled
1 cup fresh raspberries*

*To use 1 cup drained frozen or canned fruit; decrease sugar to ¼ cup.

Dissolve Jell-O Gelatin, sugar, and salt in boiling water. Add lemon juice. Set aside ½ cup for glacé. Chill remainder until slightly thickened. Fold whipped cream into the thickened gelatin. Spoon into pastry shell. Chill until set, but not firm. Meanwhile, chill the ½ cup glacé until slightly thickened. Fold in raspberries. Spread over filling in pie. Chill until firm. Garnish with additional whipped cream or prepared whipped topping, if desired.

Strawberry Glacé Pie: Prepare Raspberry Glacé Pie, substituting Jell-O Strawberry Gelatin for the raspberry gelatin and sliced or halved strawberries for the raspberries.

Cherry Glacé Pie: Prepare Raspberry Glacé Pie, substituting Jell-O Black Cherry or Cherry Gelatin for raspberry gelatin and drained canned pitted dark sweet cherries, halved, for the raspberries.

CURRANT BAVARIAN PIE

A delicately flavored pie that transforms a meal into a special occasion.

1 quart fresh currants
1 package (3 oz.) Jell-O Lemon Gelatin
½ cup boiling water
½ cup sugar

1 envelope Dream Whip Whipped Topping Mix or 1 cup whipping cream
8-inch Crumb Crust (page 32)

Cook currants over low heat until skins pop. Then press through a fine strainer or cheesecloth. (Makes about 1 cup juice.) Dissolve Jell-O Gelatin in boiling water. Stir in the currant juice and sugar. Chill until slightly thickened. Prepare whipped topping mix as directed on package, omitting vanilla, or whip the cream. Fold into gelatin mixture and chill until mixture mounds. Spoon into Crumb Crust. Chill until firm.

NOTE: If desired, omit Crumb Crust and spoon Currant Bavarian mixture into a 1½-quart mold; chill until firm. Makes about 4 cups, or 8 servings.

CHIFFON CITRUS PIE

Light, refreshing, and delicious—a pie that's a delight to serve.

3 egg yolks, slightly beaten
1½ cups water
½ cup sugar
1 package (3 oz.) Jell-O Lemon, Lime, or Orange Gelatin
3 tablespoons lemon or lime juice
1½ teaspoons grated lemon or lime rind
3 egg whites
Dash of salt
9-inch Crumb Crust (page 32)

Combine egg yolks, 1 cup water, and ¼ cup sugar in saucepan. Cook over low heat until mixture comes to a boil, stirring constantly. Remove from heat. Add Jell-O Gelatin and stir until dissolved. Add ½ cup water and the lemon juice and rind. Chill until slightly thickened.

Beat egg whites and salt until foamy. Add ¼ cup sugar, 2 tablespoons at a time, beating after each addition until blended. Then beat until mixture will stand in stiff peaks. Beat gelatin mixture slightly. Fold into meringue and again beat mixture very slightly. Pour into the Crumb Crust. Chill until firm.

Cherry Chiffon Pie: Prepare Chiffon Citrus Pie, substituting the syrup from 1 can (8¾ oz.) dark sweet cherries for the ½ cup water added with lemon juice. Set aside 4 or 5 cherries for garnish; then remove pits and halve the remaining cherries. Fold cherries into filling with meringue.

AVOCADO PIE
(Pictured below)

A pie with flair—deliciously combining avocado, pineapple, and cheese.

1 package (3 oz.) Jell-O Lime
   or Lemon Gelatin
¼ teaspoon salt
1 cup boiling water
1 can (8¾ oz.) crushed pineapple
2 tablespoons lime juice

1 medium avocado, peeled and
   halved
1 package (3 oz.) cream cheese
1 cup whipped cream or prepared
   Dream Whip Whipped Topping
9-inch Crumb Crust (page 32)

Dissolve Jell-O Gelatin and salt in boiling water. Drain pineapple, combining the syrup with lime juice; add cold water to make ¾ cup. Add to gelatin. Chill until very thick.

Meanwhile, dice half of the avocado. Mash the remaining half until smooth. Blend cheese into mashed avocado until creamy. Then fold cheese mixture, diced avocado, pineapple, and whipped cream or prepared whipped topping into thickened gelatin. Spoon into crust. Chill until firm. Garnish with drained pineapple slices or lime slices, if desired.

Avocado Pie—pineapple tops this unusually tasty avocado creation.

CHERRY WALDORF SALAD

Two-way Recipes

To serve as desserts or salads—

Prepare these recipes; then defy someone to say that you're not ready for anything. You see, you can serve them as desserts, as salads, or as snacks for the troops when they come in and demand something at the drop of a hat.

When you serve them as desserts, garnish with prepared whipped topping or whipped cream. As salads, unmold them on crisp greens and top with mayonnaise or salad dressing. Fruit mixtures, whether served as desserts or salads, spring to even more delicious, vivid life if you top them with mixtures of whipped cream and mayonnaise or sour cream and cream cheese. Aren't you kind of hungry, even now?

CHERRY WALDORF SALAD
(Pictured on opposite page)

A beautiful contrast of red gelatin with apples and banana.

    1 package (3 oz.) Jell-O Black
        Cherry or Cherry Gelatin
    Dash of salt
    1 cup boiling water
    1 cup cold water
    ½ cup diced apples
    ½ cup diced banana
    ¼ cup chopped celery

Dissolve Jell-O Gelatin and salt in boiling water. Add cold water. Chill until very thick. Fold in remaining ingredients. Spoon into a 1-quart mold, 8-inch square pan, or dessert dishes. Chill until firm. Unmold. Makes about 3 cups, or 6 servings.

Orange Waldorf Salad: Prepare Cherry Waldorf Salad, using Jell-O Lemon or Orange Gelatin instead of cherry gelatin, increasing apples to 1 cup, and substituting 1 orange, sectioned and diced, for the celery.

CREAMY PINEAPPLE SALAD

A rich, refreshing blend of sour cream and pineapple in gelatin.

    1 package (3 oz.) Jell-O Lime or
        Lemon Gelatin
    ½ teaspoon salt
    1 cup boiling water
    1 can (1 lb. 4½ oz.) crushed
        pineapple
    2 tablespoons lemon juice
    1 cup sour cream

Dissolve Jell-O Gelatin and salt in boiling water. Drain pineapple, reserving ¼ cup syrup. Add syrup, lemon juice, and sour cream to gelatin. Beat until blended. Pour into shallow pan. Place in freezer 20 to 25 minutes, or until firm 1 inch around edge and soft in center. Pour into bowl; whip until fluffy. Fold in pineapple. Pour into a 1-quart mold. Chill until firm—30 to 60 minutes. Unmold. Makes 4 cups, or 8 servings.

CRANBERRY-APPLE MOLDS

With or after a hearty meal, serve this delightful fruit salad.

1 package (3 oz.) Jell-O
    Strawberry or Mixed Fruit
    Gelatin
⅛ teaspoon salt
1¼ cups boiling water
1 can (1 lb.) jellied cranberry
    sauce
2 cups finely chopped apples

Dissolve Jell-O Gelatin and salt in boiling water. Break up cranberry sauce with fork. Add to gelatin mixture. Chill until very thick. Fold in apples. Pour into individual molds. Chill until firm. Unmold. Makes about 4 cups, or 6 to 8 servings.

AMBROSIA LOAF

A fruit combination that has been popular for many centuries.

1 can (8½ oz.) sliced pineapple
1 cup orange sections (2 oranges)*
½ cup Baker's Angel Flake Coconut
1 package (3 oz.) Jell-O Orange
    or Orange-Pineapple Gelatin
1 cup boiling water

* Or use 1 can (11 oz.) mandarin orange sections.

Drain fruits, measuring liquid. Add water to make 1 cup. Place pineapple slices in an 8x4x3-inch loaf pan or a 1-quart mold or serving dish. Add orange sections and sprinkle with the coconut. Dissolve Jell-O Gelatin in the boiling water. Stir in measured liquid. Chill until cool, but not thickened. Pour over fruits and chill until firm. Unmold or serve from the serving dish. Makes about 3½ cups, or 6 or 7 servings.

THREE-FRUIT FANTASY

For a tantalizing salad, use a bit of vinegar with the fruit. For dessert, use a little lemon juice.

1 can (8¾ oz.) crushed pineapple
1 cup diced grapefruit sections
¼ cup diced orange sections
1 package (3 oz.) Jell-O Lemon,
    Strawberry, Mixed Fruit, or
    Orange-Pineapple Gelatin
1 cup boiling water
1 tablespoon vinegar or lemon
    juice

Drain pineapple, measuring syrup. Drain grapefruit and orange sections, adding juice to pineapple syrup. Then add water to make 1 cup. Dissolve Jell-O Gelatin in boiling water. Add syrup mixture and vinegar. Chill until very thick. Fold in fruits. Pour into a 1-quart mold. Chill until firm. Unmold. Makes 4 cups, or 6 to 8 servings.

FROZEN AMBROSIA

A wonderful substitute for ice cream or sherbet that's just as refreshing.

1 package (3 oz.) Jell-O Orange-
    Pineapple or Orange Gelatin
¼ teaspoon salt
2 tablespoons sugar
1 cup boiling water
2 oranges, peeled and sectioned
1 cup whipped cream or prepared
    Dream Whip Whipped Topping
1⅓ cups (about) Baker's Angel
    Flake Coconut
1 teaspoon grated orange rind
2 tablespoons mayonnaise

Dissolve Jell-O Gelatin, salt, and sugar in boiling water. Drain orange sections, measuring juice and adding cold water to make 1 cup. Add to gelatin. Chill until very thick. Fold in whipped cream, coconut, orange sections, orange rind, and mayonnaise. Pour into freezer tray or shallow pan. Freeze until firm. Makes about 4 cups, or 6 to 8 servings.

TANGY CIDER MOLD

As refreshing as a long, cool drink of cider on a warm autumn day.

1 package (3 oz.) Jell-O Lemon
    Gelatin
1 cup boiling sweet cider
1 cup cold sweet cider

1½ cups unpeeled red apples, cut in match-stick pieces

Dissolve Jell-O Gelatin in boiling cider. Add cold cider. Chill until very thick. Then fold in apples. Spoon into serving dishes or individual molds. Chill until firm. Makes about 3 cups, or 6 servings.

Apple Ginger Mold: Prepare Tangy Cider Mold, using boiling water and cold ginger ale instead of cider.

ORANGE GINGER WHIP

A flavorful orange and ginger ale mixture that has many uses.

1 package (3 oz.) Jell-O Orange or Orange-Pineapple Gelatin
1 cup boiling ginger ale
1 cup cold orange juice*
*Or use 1 cup cold ginger ale.

Dissolve Jell-O Gelatin in boiling ginger ale. Add orange juice. Chill until very thick. Then whip until fluffy —see directions on page 84. Spoon into a 1-quart ring mold. Chill until firm. Unmold. If desired, fill center with sweetened whipped cream or prepared Dream Whip Whipped Topping and garnish with grated orange rind, orange sections, or mint leaves. Makes about 4 cups, or 4 to 6 servings.

FROSTY MELON
(Pictured below)

For a spectacular flavor combination, try lime gelatin in cantaloupe or a red gelatin in honeydew melon.

1 package (3 oz.) Jell-O Gelatin (any fruit flavor)
1 cup boiling water
¾ cup cold water or drained fruit syrup
1 medium cantaloupe or honeydew melon
1 cup drained fruit
2 or 3 packages (3 oz. each) cream cheese
2 tablespoons (about) milk

Dissolve Jell-O Gelatin in boiling water. Add cold water. Chill until very thick. Meanwhile, peel melon, leaving it whole. Cut a slice from one end, scoop out seeds, and drain well. Then place melon upright in a bowl. Fold fruit into thick gelatin; spoon into melon. Replace cut slice; fasten with toothpicks. Chill. (Pour any remaining gelatin into a small bowl, chill, and serve at another meal.)

Before serving melon, blend cream cheese and milk until smooth and fluffy. Cut a thin slice from one side of melon for a firm base; place on plate. Spread cheese over melon. Slice to serve. Makes 4 to 6 servings.

Frosty Melon—cantaloupe or honeydew filled with fruited gelatin.

FIG AND ORANGE MOLD

An unusual, delicious mold that will please everyone.

1 package (3 oz.) Jell-O Lemon, Orange, or Orange-Pineapple Gelatin
¼ teaspoon salt
1 cup boiling water
¾ cup cold water
1 tablespoon lemon juice
½ cup dried figs
1 cup diced orange sections

Dissolve Jell-O Gelatin and salt in boiling water. Add cold water and lemon juice. Chill until very thick. Meanwhile, cover figs with boiling water; let stand 10 minutes. Drain, remove stems, and cut into fine strips. Fold figs and oranges into gelatin. Pour into a 1-quart mold. Chill until firm. Unmold. Serve plain or with cream. Makes 3⅓ cups, or 6 servings.

LAYERED CHEESE AND APPLES

Fluffy cheese and apple layers are a delicious combination.

1 package (3 oz.) Jell-O Lemon or Orange Gelatin
½ teaspoon salt
1 teaspoon sugar (optional)
1 cup boiling water
¾ cup cold water
1 tablespoon lemon juice
1 cup diced red apples
1 package (3 oz.) cream cheese
½ cup chopped walnuts

Dissolve Jell-O Gelatin, salt, and sugar in boiling water. Add cold water and lemon juice. Chill until very thick. Fold apples into 1 cup gelatin. Pour into an 8-inch square pan. Chill until set, but not firm. Whip remaining gelatin until fluffy — see directions on page 84. Soften cheese, blend in a small amount of whipped gelatin, and fold into remaining whipped gelatin. Then fold in nuts. Chill until firm. Cut in slices or squares. Makes about 4½ cups, or 8 servings.

PARTY SALAD

A de luxe mold of fruit and nuts in a creamy gelatin mixture.

1 package (3 oz.) Jell-O Lemon or Lime Gelatin
1 cup boiling water
1 can (1 lb. 4½ oz.) crushed pineapple
½ cup cottage cheese
1 cup whipped cream or prepared Dream Whip Whipped Topping
¼ cup chopped maraschino cherries
¼ cup chopped blanched almonds

Dissolve Jell-O Gelatin in boiling water. Drain pineapple, measuring ½ cup syrup. Add to gelatin. Chill until very thick. Fold in pineapple, cheese, whipped cream, cherries, and almonds. Pour into individual molds or a 9x5x3-inch loaf pan. Chill until firm. Unmold. Makes 4½ cups, or 8 servings.

RICHELIEU MOLDS

These vivid red molds are traditionally served with an almond topping.

1 package (3 oz.) Jell-O Cherry Gelatin
1 cup boiling water
1 can (1 lb. 1 oz.) pitted dark sweet cherries
2 tablespoons orange juice
¾ cup diced orange sections
Toasted Almond Topping

Dissolve Jell-O Gelatin in boiling water. Drain cherries, measuring syrup. Add cold water to make ¾ cup. Add cherry syrup and orange juice to gelatin. Chill until very thick. Fold in cherries and oranges. Pour into individual molds. Chill until firm. Unmold. Serve with the topping. Makes 4 cups, or 6 to 8 servings.

Toasted Almond Topping: For salads, combine ½ cup whipped cream, ½ cup mayonnaise, and ¼ cup chopped toasted almonds. For desserts, combine 1 cup whipped cream and ¼ cup chopped toasted almonds.

AVOCADO STRAWBERRY RING
(Pictured below)

*It's a delight to serve a light green
and vivid red delicacy.*

1 package (3 oz.) Jell-O Lemon
  or Lime Gelatin
½ teaspoon salt
1 cup boiling water
¾ cup cold water
1 tablespoon lemon juice
1 avocado, pared and mashed
3 tablespoons mayonnaise
1 pint fresh strawberries*

* Or use 2 packages (10 oz. each) Birds Eye
Strawberries, thawed and drained.

Dissolve Jell-O Gelatin and salt in
boiling water. Add cold water. Chill
until slightly thickened. Stir lemon
juice into avocado; blend into gelatin
with mayonnaise. Pour into a 3- or
4-cup ring mold or individual ring
molds. Chill until firm. Unmold; fill
center with berries. Makes about 2½
cups gelatin, or 5 servings.

CITRUS SURPRISE
(Pictured below)

*A citrus mold that's delicious and
versatile. It's even good for breakfast.*

¾ cup orange sections
¾ cup grapefruit sections
1 package (3 oz.) Jell-O Gelatin
  (any fruit flavor)
⅛ teaspoon salt
1 cup boiling water

Sweeten fruit to taste; set aside. Dissolve Jell-O Gelatin and salt in boiling water. Drain fruit, measuring
juice and adding water to make ¾
cup. Add juice to gelatin. Chill 1 cup
of the mixture until very thick. Then
whip until fluffy — see directions on
page 84. Pour into a 1-quart mold.
Chill until set, but not firm. Chill remaining gelatin until very thick;
then fold in fruit. Spoon into mold.
Chill until firm. Unmold and garnish
with mint and sour cream, if desired.
Makes about 3½ cups, or 6 servings.

Avocado Strawberry Ring, Citrus Surprise, and Ribbon Salad (page 46).

FRUITED SPECIAL

A fruit salad with just a touch of tartness to bring out flavors.

  1 package (3 oz.) Jell-O Raspberry, Strawberry-Banana, or Mixed Fruit Gelatin
  1 cup boiling water
  ½ cup cold water
  1 package (10 oz.) Birds Eye Red Raspberries or Strawberries
  1 tablespoon lemon juice
  1 medium banana, sliced

Dissolve Jell-O Gelatin in boiling water. Add cold water and frozen fruit, stirring until fruit separates. Add lemon juice. Chill until very thick. Fold in banana. Pour into individual molds or a 1-quart mold. Chill until firm. Unmold. Makes about 3 cups, or 6 servings.

FRUIT COCKTAIL SALAD

A recipe you can change at will—almost any canned fruit may be used.

  1 package (3 oz.) Jell-O Gelatin (any fruit flavor)
  1 cup boiling water
  1 can (1 lb. 1 oz.) fruit cocktail
  1 tablespoon lemon juice
  ¼ cup coarsely chopped nuts
  1 banana, sliced

Dissolve Jell-O Gelatin in boiling water. Drain fruit, measuring ¾ cup syrup. Add syrup and lemon juice to gelatin. Chill until very thick. Then fold in fruit and nuts. Pour into a 1-quart mold or bowl or individual molds. Chill until firm. Unmold. Makes about 3½ cups, or 6 servings.

LAYERED ORANGE TREAT

A refreshing dessert that's just as tasty served as a salad.

  2 packages (3 oz. each) Jell-O Orange or Orange-Pineapple Gelatin
  2 cups boiling water
  1 pint orange sherbet

  1 can (11 oz.) mandarin orange sections*

*Or use 1 cup diced fresh oranges and 1 cup cold water.

Dissolve 1 package Jell-O Gelatin in 1 cup boiling water. Blend in sherbet. Pour into a 1½-quart mold. Freeze until firm. Dissolve remaining Jell-O Gelatin in remaining boiling water. Drain orange sections, measuring syrup; add cold water to make 1 cup. Add syrup mixture and orange sections to gelatin. Pour over frozen layer. Chill until firm, at least 30 minutes. Unmold on lettuce, if desired. Makes 5¾ cups, or 8 to 10 servings.

NOTE: The frozen layer may be made ahead and stored in freezer a week or two. Then add the second layer at least 30 minutes before serving salad.

Lime Treat: Prepare Layered Orange Treat, substituting Jell-O Lime Gelatin and lime sherbet for the orange gelatin and sherbet and 1 can (8¾ oz.) white grapes for the mandarin orange sections.

DOUBLE RASPBERRY SALAD

A double treat for raspberry-lovers, plus a bonus of melon.

  1 package (10 oz.) Birds Eye Red Raspberries, thawed
  1 tablespoon lemon juice
  1¾ cups cantaloupe or honeydew melon balls
  1 package (3 oz.) Jell-O Raspberry or Black Raspberry Gelatin
  ¼ teaspoon salt
  1 cup boiling water

Drain berries, measuring syrup; add water to make ¾ cup liquid. Sprinkle lemon juice over melon balls. Dissolve Jell-O Gelatin and salt in boiling water. Stir in syrup mixture. Chill until very thick. Fold in raspberries and 1 cup melon balls. Pour into 1-quart mold or individual molds. Chill until firm. Unmold; garnish with remaining melon. Makes about 3¾ cups, or 6 or 7 servings.

Minty Pear Cheese Salad—pears and cream cheese in lime gelatin.

MINTY PEAR CHEESE SALAD
(Pictured above)

A taste-treat that compliments the rest of the menu perfectly.

**2 packages (3 oz. each) or 1 package (6 oz.) Jell-O Lime Gelatin
⅛ teaspoon salt
2 cups boiling water
1 can (1 lb.) pear halves
8 drops mint extract
2 packages (3 oz. each) cream cheese, softened**

Dissolve Jell-O Gelatin and salt in boiling water. Drain pears, measuring syrup and adding water to make 1¾ cups. Stir syrup and extract into gelatin. Set aside 1 cup gelatin; pour remainder into a 9x5x3-inch loaf pan or a 1½-quart mold. Chill until slightly thickened. Then quarter pear halves and place in gelatin. Chill until set, but not firm. Gradually blend the 1 cup gelatin into cream cheese; pour into the pan. Chill until firm. Unmold on salad greens and serve with sour cream, if desired. Makes about 5½ cups, or 10 servings.

Minty Pear Salad: Prepare Minty Pear Cheese Salad, omitting the cream cheese, pouring all of the gelatin into the pan, and chilling until thickened before adding the pears.

MAGIC-LAYER MOLD

Blender-made, self-layering gelatin— a clear layer forms at bottom.

**1 package (3 oz.) Jell-O Gelatin (any fruit flavor)
¾ cup boiling water
1½ cups crushed ice
1 banana, sliced**

Combine Jell-O Gelatin and boiling water in blender container. Cover; blend at low speed 30 seconds, or until gelatin dissolves. Add ice; blend at high speed until ice melts—about 30 seconds. Pour into a 1-quart mold; stir in banana. Chill at least 1 hour. (A clear bottom layer forms during chilling.) Unmold. Makes 4 cups, or 6 to 8 servings.

Magic Avocado Mold. Prepare Magic-Layer Mold with lemon gelatin, adding ½ teaspoon salt and 1 tablespoon lemon juice and substituting 1 avocado, diced, for the banana.

Magic Cherry Dessert. Drain 1 package (10 oz.) Birds Eye Sweet Cherries, thawed, reserving syrup. Add water to make ¾ cup liquid; bring to a boil. Prepare Magic-Layer Mold with cherry gelatin, using cherry syrup instead of water and adding 3 tablespoons red port wine with ice; omit banana. Pour into 8 wine glasses; add about 5 cherries to each glass. Chill at least 15 minutes.

APPLESAUCE DE LUXE

A most versatile recipe—use it as dessert, salad, or relish.

**1 package (3 oz.) Jell-O Raspberry or Cherry Gelatin
1 cup boiling water
1½ cups (15-oz. jar) applesauce
1 teaspoon lemon juice**

Dissolve Jell-O Gelatin in boiling water. Blend in applesauce and lemon juice. Pour into individual molds or a serving dish. Chill until firm. Unmold. Serve with sour cream or mayonnaise, if desired. Makes about 2½ cups, or 5 to 7 servings.

DE LUXE CHEESE MOLD

Corresponding flavors of gelatin and sherbet compliment cottage cheese.

1 package (3 oz.) Jell-O Orange-Pineapple or Orange Gelatin*
1 cup boiling water
1 cup orange sherbet*
1½ cups cottage cheese with pineapple

*Or use any other corresponding flavors of Jell-O Gelatin and sherbet.

Dissolve Jell-O Gelatin in boiling water. Blend in sherbet. Chill until very thick. Stir in cottage cheese. Spoon into individual molds or a 1-quart mold. Chill until firm. Serve with sour cream, if desired. Makes 3½ cups, or about 6 servings.

NOTE: If desired, use 1 cup plain cottage cheese and add 1 can (8¾ oz.) drained crushed pineapple.

TAHITIAN DELIGHT

Savor the delights of the South Seas in this easy mold.

1 package (3 oz.) Jell-O Cherry, Orange, or Lime Gelatin
1 cup boiling water
1 can (8¾ oz.) crushed pineapple
1 small banana, sliced
½ cup Baker's Angel Flake Coconut or chopped nuts

Dissolve Jell-O Gelatin in boiling water. Drain pineapple, measuring syrup. Add water to make ¾ cup; add to gelatin. Chill until very thick. Then fold in fruit and coconut. Pour into individual molds. Chill until firm. Unmold. Makes 3½ cups, or 6 servings.

BANANA PEANUT SALAD

Children—of all ages—will enjoy it with, after, and between meals.

1 package (3 oz.) Jell-O Lime, Orange, or Strawberry-Banana Gelatin
1 cup boiling water
1 cup cold water
1 banana, sliced

2 tablespoons mayonnaise
2 tablespoons chopped salted peanuts

Dissolve Jell-O Gelatin in boiling water. Add cold water. Chill until very thick. Measure 1 cup gelatin and add banana. Spoon into individual molds. Chill until set, but not firm. Meanwhile, blend mayonnaise into remaining gelatin; add peanuts. Spoon into molds. Chill until firm. Unmold. Makes 3 cups, or 6 servings.

CHERRY SUPREME

The Marshmallow-Mayonnaise Topping served on this cherry mold is also delicious on other salads.

1 package (3 oz.) Jell-O Cherry or Black Cherry Gelatin
2 tablespoons sugar
Dash of salt
1 cup boiling water
1 can (1 lb. 1 oz.) pitted dark sweet cherries
1 tablespoon lemon juice
½ cup whipped cream or prepared Dream Whip Whipped Topping
1 cup diced or miniature marshmallows
Marshmallow-Mayonnaise Topping

Dissolve Jell-O Gelatin, sugar, and salt in boiling water. Drain cherries, measuring syrup. Add water to make ¾ cup. Add syrup and lemon juice to gelatin. Chill until very thick. Then fold half of the cherries into 1 cup gelatin. Pour into a 1-quart mold. Chill until set, but not firm. Meanwhile, whip remaining gelatin until fluffy—see directions on page 84. Then fold in cream, remaining cherries, and marshmallows. Spoon into mold. Chill until firm. Unmold; serve with Marshmallow-Mayonnaise Topping. Makes about 4 cups, or 8 servings.

Marshmallow-Mayonnaise Topping: Blend ⅓ cup marshmallow cream into ⅔ cup mayonnaise, stirring until smooth. Makes 1 cup.

CITRUS RING

Sweetened orange and grapefruit sections release some of their delicious juice for use in the gelatin.

1 cup diced orange sections
1 cup diced grapefruit sections
¼ cup sugar
1 package (3 oz.) Jell-O Orange or Orange-Pineapple Gelatin
1 cup boiling water
1 tablespoon grated orange rind
3 tablespoons chopped maraschino cherries
⅓ cup Baker's Angel Flake or Premium Shred Coconut

Combine orange sections, grapefruit sections, and sugar; let stand 10 minutes. Then dissolve Jell-O Gelatin in boiling water. Drain sweetened fruit, measuring juice and adding water to make ¾ cup. Add juice mixture and orange rind to gelatin. Chill until very thick. Then fold in orange, grapefruit, cherries, and coconut. Spoon into a 1-quart ring mold or individual molds. Chill until firm. Unmold. Garnish with sweetened whipped cream or prepared Dream Whip Whipped Topping and mint leaves, if desired. Makes about 4 cups, or 6 to 8 servings.

RED CURRANT MOLDS

Enjoy the short currant season with a mold that fairly bursts with flavor.

2 cups stemmed washed fresh red currants
½ cup sugar
1 cup water
1 package (3 oz.) Jell-O Raspberry or Cherry Gelatin

Cook currants with sugar and water over medium heat until skins pop, stirring occasionally. Then force through fine sieve. Add Jell-O Gelatin to strained fruit and stir until dissolved. Pour into individual molds. Chill until firm. Unmold. Serve with a dollop of sour cream, if desired. Makes about 2 cups, or 4 servings.

GINGERED-PEAR MOLD

Pear slices chilled in ginger-flavored juice make an extra-tasty mold.

2 packages (3 oz. each) Jell-O Strawberry Punch or Lemon Gelatin
2 tablespoons sugar
½ teaspoon ground ginger
2 cups boiling water
1 can (1 lb.) sliced pears
Cold water or ginger ale

Combine Jell-O Gelatin, sugar, ginger, and boiling water; stir until gelatin is dissolved. Drain pears, measuring syrup. Add cold water to syrup to make 1½ cups; add to gelatin. Pour a thin layer into an 8-inch layer pan; chill until set, but not firm. Chill remaining gelatin until thickened. Arrange pears on gelatin in pan; spoon thickened gelatin over pears. Chill until firm. Unmold. Makes about 4 cups, or 8 servings.

CREAM-TOPPED PEACHES

Choose your favorite, cream cheese or sour cream, for one of these layers.

1 package (3 oz.) Jell-O Lime, Mixed Fruit, or Strawberry-Banana Gelatin
2 tablespoons sugar
⅛ teaspoon salt
1 cup boiling water
1 can (8¾ oz.) sliced peaches
2 teaspoons lime or lemon juice
1 package (3 oz.) cream cheese, softened*
*Or use ½ cup sour cream.

Dissolve Jell-O Gelatin, sugar, and salt in boiling water. Drain peaches, measuring syrup. Add water to make 1 cup. Stir syrup and lime juice into gelatin. Gradually blend ½ cup gelatin into cheese. Pour into an 8x4x2-inch loaf pan or a 1-quart mold. Chill until set, but not firm. Meanwhile, chill remaining gelatin until very thick. Stir in peaches. Spoon into mold. Chill until firm. Cut in squares or unmold. Makes about 3 cups, or 6 servings.

RIBBON SALAD
(Pictured on page 41)

"Tie up" your meal with a lovely and delicious ribbon of gelatin.

1 package (3 oz.) <u>each</u> Jell-O Lemon, Lime, <u>and</u> Raspberry Gelatins
3 cups boiling water
1 cup miniature or diced marshmallows
1½ cups cold water
2 packages (3 oz. each) cream cheese, softened
½ cup mayonnaise
1 cup whipped cream
1 can (1 lb. 4½ oz.) crushed pineapple

Dissolve Jell-O Gelatin flavors separately, using 1 cup boiling water for each. Stir marshmallows into lemon gelatin; set aside. Add ¾ cup cold water to lime gelatin; pour into a 13x9x2-inch pan. Chill until set, but not firm. Add ¾ cup cold water to raspberry gelatin; set aside at room temperature. Then add cream cheese to lemon mixture; beat until blended. Chill until slightly thickened. Then blend in mayonnaise, whipped cream, and crushed pineapple. Chill until very thick; spoon gently over lime gelatin. Chill until set, but not firm. Meanwhile, chill raspberry gelatin until thickened; pour over lemon gelatin. Chill until firm. To serve, cut in squares. Makes about 10 cups, or 12 to 15 servings.

NOTE: If deeper green and red layers are desired, use 6-oz. packages Jell-O Lime and Raspberry Gelatins and 2 cups boiling water and 1½ cups cold water for <u>each</u> large package.

THREE-LAYER FRUIT MOLD

Layer three fruits in a pan, add gelatin, and you're done!

2 packages (3 oz. each) or 1 package (6 oz.) Jell-O Lime Gelatin
2 cups boiling water
1 can (1 lb.) apricot halves
1 can (1 lb.) pear halves
2 bananas, sliced

Dissolve Jell-O Gelatin in boiling water. Drain canned fruits, measuring 1½ cups syrup; add to gelatin. Layer apricot halves and pear halves in a 9x5x3-inch loaf pan or a 2-quart mold. Top with sliced bananas. Pour gelatin over fruits. Chill until firm. Unmold. Makes 8 cups, or 12 to 14 servings.

NOTE: A 1-lb. or 1-lb. 4½-oz. can of peach halves or slices, pineapple slices, or fruit cocktail may be substituted for the fruit suggested in recipe.

MINT-GLAZED PEARS
(Pictured below)

Here's an easy way to turn canned pears into an elegant dessert.

1 can (1 lb.) pear halves, drained
1 package (3 oz.) Jell-O Lime Gelatin
1 cup boiling water
½ teaspoon mint extract

Arrange pear halves in skillet. Dissolve gelatin in boiling water. Add mint extract. Then pour over pears. Broil, basting often, until glaze begins to bubble and pears are lightly tinted —about 15 minutes. Serve warm or chilled. Makes 5 to 8 glazed pear halves, or 3 or 4 servings.

Mint-Glazed Pears—the glaze is lime gelatin flavored with mint.

Frozen Fruit Salad—an ever-popular, refreshing dessert or salad.

FROZEN FRUIT SALAD
(Pictured above)

A lovely, delicious frozen salad that can also be a beautiful dessert.

- 1 package (3 oz.) Jell-O Mixed Fruit, Strawberry, Lemon, or Orange-Pineapple Gelatin
- Dash of salt
- 1 cup boiling water
- 1 can (8¾ oz.) pineapple tidbits
- ¼ cup lemon juice
- ⅓ cup mayonnaise
- 1 cup whipping cream*
- 1 medium banana, diced
- ½ cup seeded halved grapes
- ¼ cup diced maraschino cherries
- ¼ cup chopped nuts

*Or use 2 cups sour cream.

Dissolve Jell-O Gelatin and salt in boiling water. Drain pineapple, measuring syrup; add water to make ½ cup, if necessary. Stir into gelatin with lemon juice. Blend in mayonnaise. Chill until very thick. Whip cream. Fold fruits, nuts, and whipped cream into gelatin. Pour into 2 freezing trays or a 9x5x3-inch loaf pan. Freeze until firm—at least 3 to 4 hours. To serve, cut in squares or slices. Makes about 4½ cups, or 8 servings.

NOTE: Other fruits that may be used in the Frozen Fruit Salad are: drained diced orange sections, drained canned crushed pineapple, or drained canned fruit cocktail, using a total of about 2 cups fruit.

CANTALOUPE-NUT SALAD

Slivered almonds and celery add texture to this layered mold.

- 1 package (3 oz.) Jell-O Orange, Lemon, or Lime Gelatin
- Dash of salt
- 1 cup boiling water
- ¾ cup cold water
- 1 teaspoon lemon juice
- 1 cup diced cantaloupe or small cantaloupe balls
- ¼ cup sliced celery
- ¼ cup finely slivered almonds
- 1 package (3 oz.) cream cheese
- 2 tablespoons mayonnaise

Dissolve Jell-O Gelatin and salt in boiling water. Add cold water and lemon juice. Chill half the gelatin until very thick. Fold in cantaloupe, celery, and almonds. Pour into a shallow pan or individual molds. Chill until set, but not firm. Mix cheese and mayonnaise until smooth. Gradually blend in remaining gelatin. Pour over layer in pan. Chill until firm. Unmold on crisp greens. Serve with cream cheese balls, additional mayonnaise, or sour cream, if desired. Makes about 4 cups, or 6 to 8 servings.

Peach and Cheese Salad—layers of sliced peaches and cottage cheese.

RASPBERRY PINEAPPLE MOLD

A delightful fruit combination to use as salad or dessert.

- 2 packages (3 oz. each) Jell-O Orange or Orange-Pineapple Gelatin
- 2 cups boiling water
- 1 cup cold water
- 1 package (10 oz.) Birds Eye Red Raspberries
- 1 can (13½ oz.) pineapple tidbits

Dissolve Jell-O Gelatin in boiling water. Add cold water. Stir in frozen fruit until berries are separated. Add undrained pineapple tidbits. Chill until very thick. Then stir to distribute fruits evenly. Pour into 9x5x3-inch loaf pan or 1½-quart mold. Chill until firm. Makes 5 cups, or 10 servings.

Strawberry Pineapple Mold: Prepare Raspberry Pineapple Mold, substituting Jell-O Strawberry Gelatin for orange gelatin and Birds Eye Strawberries for raspberries.

PEACH AND CHEESE SALAD
(Pictured at left)

A creamy cottage cheese mixture is set off by a beautiful peach layer.

- 1 package (3 oz.) Jell-O Cherry Gelatin
- Dash of salt
- 1 cup boiling water
- ¾ cup cold water
- 1¼ cups sweetened sliced fresh peaches*
- 1½ cups cottage cheese

*Or use drained canned or frozen peaches.

Dissolve Jell-O Gelatin and salt in boiling water. Add cold water. Chill until very thick. Fold peaches into 1 cup gelatin. Pour into a 1½-quart ring mold. Chill until set, but not firm. Beat cottage cheese until smooth. Whip remaining gelatin until fluffy—see directions on page 84. Fold in cheese. Pour into mold. Chill until firm. Unmold. If desired, fill ring with more cottage cheese and sliced peaches. Makes about 6 cups, or 8 to 10 servings.

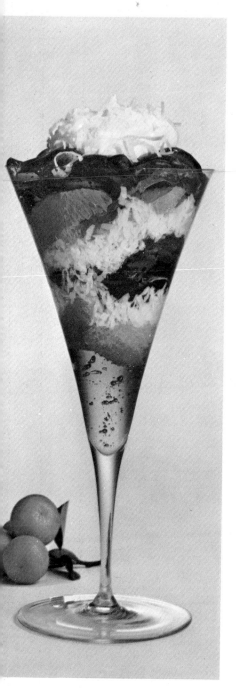

Ambrosia Parfaits—delightful tiers of fruit, gelatin, and coconut.

ORANGE AND GRAPE DUO

The fruits for this dazzler are available any season of the year.

> 2 oranges
> 1 package (3 oz.) Jell-O Orange-Pineapple, Orange, Lime, or Strawberry Gelatin
> 1 tablespoon sugar
> 1 cup boiling water
> 1 cup whipped cream or prepared Dream Whip Whipped Topping
> 1¼ cups seeded halved red grapes*
> ⅔ cup Baker's Angel Flake Coconut (optional)

*Or use halved seedless green grapes or 2 bananas, diced.

Section oranges; set aside. Dissolve Jell-O Gelatin and sugar in boiling water. Then drain oranges, measuring juice and adding water to make ¾ cup; add to gelatin. Chill until slightly thickened. Blend in whipped cream or prepared whipped topping. Chill until very thick. Fold in fruit and coconut. Spoon into a 1½-quart mold. Chill until firm. Unmold. Makes about 4½ cups, or 8 servings.

Ambrosia Parfaits: (Pictured at left) Prepare Orange and Grape Duo, chilling gelatin after adding juice until very thick; then layer gelatin, oranges, and coconut in parfait glasses or goblets. Omit grapes. Chill until firm. Garnish with the whipped cream.

GINGER-UPPER

Even weight-watchers can enjoy this delight—only 93 calories per serving.

> 1 package (3 oz.) Jell-O Gelatin (any fruit flavor)
> 1 cup boiling water
> 1½ teaspoons lemon juice
> 1 cup ginger ale
> 1 cup diced fresh pears

Dissolve Jell-O Gelatin in boiling water. Add lemon juice and ginger ale. Chill until very thick. Add pears. Spoon into molds. Chill until firm. Unmold. Makes 3 cups, or 6 servings.

(From top to bottom)

SEA DREAM (page 66)

VEGETABLE TRIO (opposite page)

VEGETABLE TRIO
(Pictured on opposite page)

A dazzling, delicious rainbow of fresh vegetables for your dinner table.

> 2 packages (3 oz. each) or
> 1 package (6 oz.) Jell-O
> Lemon Gelatin
> 1 tablespoon salt
> 2 cups boiling water
> 2 cups cold water
> 2 tablespoons vinegar
> 1½ cups finely shredded carrots
> 1¾ cups finely shredded cabbage
> 1 teaspoon minced chives
> 1½ cups finely chopped spinach

Dissolve Jell-O Gelatin and salt in boiling water. Add cold water and vinegar. Chill until slightly thickened. Divide into three portions. Fold carrots into one portion; pour into a 9x5x3-inch loaf pan. Chill until set, but not firm. Fold cabbage into second portion. Pour into pan; chill until set, but not firm. Fold chives and spinach into remaining gelatin. Pour into pan. Chill until firm. Unmold. Slice and garnish with crisp greens. Makes about 6 cups, or 12 side salads.

TANGY CABBAGE SALAD

A flavorful, softly-set vegetable relish to serve with meats.

> 1 package (3 oz.) Jell-O Lemon, Lime, or Orange Gelatin
> ½ teaspoon salt
> 1 cup boiling water
> 1½ cups cold water
> 2 teaspoons vinegar
> 2 tablespoons prepared horse-radish
> 1½ cups shredded cabbage
> 1 tablespoon chopped pimiento
> ¼ cup chopped dill pickle
> 3 drops tabasco sauce

Dissolve Jell-O Gelatin and salt in boiling water. Add cold water and vinegar. Chill until slightly thickened; add remaining ingredients. Pour into serving bowl; chill. Makes 3 cups, or 6 to 8 relish servings.

$\mathcal{S}alads$

To serve with meals or as main dishes—

Salads are more than lettuce and a radish or two when they are made with Jell-O Gelatin. Tangy gelatin molds enliven the taste of the vegetables, fruits, and other ingredients you add. Serve them with meat, fish, or poultry. Add salad greens and mayonnaise or sour cream. A Jell-O Gelatin salad is a delicious, refreshing complement for every menu.

WALDORF MOLD

This tasty salad is a lovely luncheon entree with cold cuts and hot muffins.

1 package (3 oz.) Jell-O Lemon, Mixed Fruit, or Orange-Pineapple Gelatin
½ teaspoon salt
1 cup boiling water
¾ cup cold water
2 teaspoons vinegar
¾ cup finely diced celery*
1 cup diced red apples
¼ cup chopped walnuts
¼ cup mayonnaise (optional)

***Or use ¾ cup halved seeded red grapes.**

Dissolve Jell-O Gelatin and salt in boiling water. Add cold water and vinegar. Chill until very thick. Fold in celery, apples, walnuts, and mayonnaise. Spoon into individual molds or a 1-quart mold. Chill until firm. Unmold and serve with cheese balls (see Note), if desired. Makes 3⅓ cups, or 6 side salads or 3 entree servings.

NOTE: To make cheese balls, shape a 3-oz. package cream cheese into 12 small balls. Roll in chopped nuts.

Easy Waldorf Mold: Dissolve 1 package (3 oz.) Jell-O Lemon, Lime, or Mixed Fruit Gelatin in 1 cup boiling water; then add ¾ cup cold water. Chill until very thick. Then fold in 1½ cups prepared Waldorf salad (homemade or commercial). Pour into a 1-quart mold. Chill until firm.

CRAB APPLE SALAD

Beautiful red molds that compliment any menu with tart-sweet flavor.

1 jar (1 lb.) spiced crab apples
1 package (3 oz.) Jell-O Cherry, Strawberry, or Mixed Fruit Gelatin
1 cup boiling water
1 tablespoon grated orange rind

Dissolve Jell-O Gelatin in boiling water. Drain crab apples, measuring ¾ cup syrup; add water, if necessary. Add crab apple syrup to gelatin.

Chill until very thick. Then chop the apples; fold into gelatin with orange rind. Pour into individual molds or a 1-quart mold. Chill until firm. Unmold on crisp lettuce. Serve with sour cream or mayonnaise, if desired. Makes 3 cups, or 12 side salads.

SUMMER SALAD
(Pictured on page 61)

A delicious, lovely salad that displays the bounty of the season.

1 package (3 oz.) Jell-O Lemon Gelatin
½ teaspoon salt or onion salt
1 cup boiling water
¾ cup cold water
1 tablespoon vinegar
1 small tomato, cut into thin wedges
¼ cup sliced celery
¼ cup sliced quartered cucumber
Few slivers green pepper
Dash of oregano (optional)

Dissolve Jell-O Gelatin and salt in boiling water. Add cold water and vinegar. Chill until very thick. Fold in remaining ingredients. Pour into a 3-cup or 1-quart mold. Chill until firm. Unmold on crisp greens. Garnish with more tomato, if desired. Makes about 3 cups, or 6 side salads.

NOTE: If desired, substitute ½ cup sliced radishes for tomato or ½ cup chopped cauliflower for cucumber.

APPLE CHEESE SALAD

A tangy, satisfying mold to serve as a side salad or a luncheon entree. For a heartier meal, try the tuna version.

1 package (3 oz.) Jell-O Lemon or Lime Gelatin
½ teaspoon salt
1 cup boiling water
¾ cup cold water
1 tablespoon lemon juice
Dash of pepper
1½ cups cottage cheese
¾ cup diced unpeeled tart apples
¼ cup chopped pecans

Apple Tuna Mold—a beautiful, satisfying entree for a cool meal.

Dissolve Jell-O Gelatin and salt in boiling water. Add cold water, lemon juice, and pepper. Chill until very thick. Fold in cheese, apples, and pecans. Pour into a 1-quart mold or individual molds. Chill until firm. Unmold. Makes about 4 cups, or 4 entree servings or 6 to 8 side salads.

Apple Tuna Mold: (Pictured above) Prepare Apple Cheese Salad, increasing diced apples to 1 cup and substituting 1 can (7 oz.) flaked drained tuna and ½ cup chopped celery for the cheese and pecans; pour into a 2-quart mold. Chill until set, but not firm. Prepare 1 package (3 oz.) Jell-O Lemon or Lime Gelatin as directed on package; chill until very thick. Whip —see directions on page 84; spoon into mold. Chill; unmold. Makes 8 cups, or 6 entree salads.

MOLDED HOMEMADE SALADS

Use fruit flavor gelatin to keep your salads—such as potato and apple salads, cole slaw, and meat, fish, and poultry salads—fresh and flavorful anytime you make them in advance.

Prepare Jell-O Lemon, Lime, Orange, or Orange-Pineapple Gelatin* as directed on package, using a 3-oz. package for 3 to 6 cups of salad, or one 6-oz. package for 6 to 10 cups of salad. For firmer salads, use only ½ cup cold water for each 3 oz. of gelatin. Chill until thick. Then combine salad and gelatin. Chill until serving time, or until firm. To store salads overnight or longer, cover to prevent evaporation and drying.

*For fruit salads, use Jell-O Strawberry, Raspberry, Mixed Fruit, or Cherry Gelatin.

FRUITED PERFECTION

An interestingly flavored salad—consommé replaces part of the water.

1 can (10½ oz.) condensed consommé
1 package (3 oz.) Jell-O Lemon, Lime, or Orange-Pineapple Gelatin
¾ cup water
1 tablespoon vinegar
2 tablespoons sliced stuffed green olives
1 can (8¾ oz.) pineapple tidbits, drained
¾ cup shredded cabbage
⅓ cup chopped walnuts

Bring consommé to a boil. Stir in Jell-O Gelatin until dissolved. Add water and vinegar. Chill until very thick. Spoon a small amount into a 1-quart mold. Top with a few olive slices. Stir remaining ingredients into remaining gelatin. Spoon into mold. Chill until firm. Unmold. Makes 3¾ cups, or 6 to 8 side salads.

CREAM-TOP SALADS

A popular carrot and pineapple combination, plus a sour cream layer.

2 packages (3 oz. each) Jell-O Lemon or Orange-Pineapple Gelatin
½ teaspoon salt
2 cups boiling water
1 tablespoon lemon juice
½ cup sour cream
¾ cup cold water
1 cup shredded carrots
1 can (8¾ oz.) pineapple tidbits

Dissolve Jell-O Gelatin and salt in boiling water. Add lemon juice. To ½ cup gelatin, add sour cream and ¼ cup cold water. Pour into 1½-quart mold; chill until set, but not firm. Mix remaining gelatin and cold water, carrots, and pineapple. Chill until slightly thickened. Pour into mold. Chill until firm. Unmold. Makes 6 cups, or 12 side salads.

CAULIFLOWER RADISH SALAD

A colorful jewel of a salad that will crown your meal regally.

1 package (3 oz.) Jell-O Lemon or Lime Gelatin
½ teaspoon salt
1 cup boiling water
¾ cup cold water
1 cup diced red radishes
¾ cup chopped raw cauliflower
4 teaspoons vinegar
1 teaspoon grated onion

Dissolve Jell-O Gelatin and salt in boiling water. Add cold water. Chill until very thick. Combine remaining ingredients; let stand 20 minutes to marinate. Fold into gelatin. Pour into individual molds. Chill until firm. Unmold on salad greens. Makes about 3½ cups, or 6 side salads.

VEGETABLES IN SOUR CREAM

A well-seasoned salad, fairly bursting with crisp vegetables.

1 package (3 oz.) Jell-O Lemon or Lime Gelatin
2 bouillon cubes
1 cup boiling water
1 cup sour cream
2 tablespoons tarragon vinegar
¾ cup diced celery
½ cup thinly sliced radishes
½ cup diced cucumber
¼ cup green pepper strips
2 tablespoons thinly sliced scallions
½ teaspoon salt
Dash of pepper

Dissolve Jell-O Gelatin and bouillon cubes in boiling water. Chill until very thick. Add remaining ingredients. Pour into a 1-quart mold or individual molds. Chill until firm. Unmold on crisp lettuce. Makes 3¾ cups, or 6 to 8 side salads.

NOTE: If desired, substitute 1 package (10 oz.) Birds Eye Peas and Carrots, cooked and drained, for radishes, cucumber, and green pepper.

UNDER-THE-SEA SALAD

Pears and cream cheese lie beneath a clear sea-green layer after unmolding.

1 package (3 oz.) Jell-O Lime Gelatin
¼ teaspoon salt   1 cup boiling water
1 can (1 lb.) pear halves   1 tablespoon lemon juice
2 packages (3 oz. each) cream cheese   ⅛ teaspoon ginger

Dissolve Jell-O Gelatin and salt in boiling water. Drain pears, measuring ¾ cup syrup; add water, if necessary. Dice pears and set aside. Add pear syrup and lemon juice to gelatin. Measure 1¼ cups into a 1-quart mold. Chill until set, but not firm.

Meanwhile, soften cheese until creamy. Gradually add remaining gelatin, blending until smooth. Add ginger. Chill until very thick. Fold in pears. Spoon into mold. Chill until firm. Unmold on crisp lettuce. Makes about 4 cups, or 8 side salads.

HAWAIIAN EYEFUL

Sweet pineapple, tangy oranges, and crisp celery make a tempting salad.

2 packages (3 oz. each)
Jell-O Orange-Pineapple or
Orange Gelatin
¾ teaspoon salt
2 cups boiling water
1 can (13½ oz.) pineapple tidbits
1 teaspoon vinegar
1 cup diced orange sections
1 cup chopped celery

Dissolve Jell-O Gelatin and salt in boiling water. Drain pineapple, measuring syrup; add water to make 1½ cups. Stir syrup and vinegar into gelatin. Chill until very thick. Then stir in fruit and celery. Pour into a 1½-quart mold. Chill until firm. Unmold on lettuce. Makes about 6 cups, or 12 side salads.

GRAPEFRUIT SALAD

A tart mold of grapefruit perks up the most humdrum lunch or dinner.

1 package (3 oz.) Jell-O Lemon or
Orange-Pineapple Gelatin
¼ teaspoon salt
1 cup boiling water
1½ cups diced grapefruit sections

Dissolve Jell-O Gelatin and salt in boiling water. Drain grapefruit, measuring juice. Add water to make ¾ cup; add to gelatin. Chill until very thick. Fold in grapefruit. Pour into individual molds. Chill until firm. Unmold. Makes 3 cups, or 6 side salads.

Grapefruit Celery Salad: Prepare Grapefruit Salad, reducing diced grapefruit to 1 cup and adding 1 tablespoon lemon juice and ¼ cup mayonnaise with the juices and 1 cup diced celery with the grapefruit.

Grapefruit Cabbage Salad: Prepare Grapefruit Salad, reducing diced grapefruit to 1 cup and adding 1 tablespoon lemon juice, 1 tablespoon prepared horse-radish, 1 cup shredded cabbage, and ¼ cup sliced olives.

ORANGE RAISIN SALAD

A delectable mold—especially refreshing with ham or chicken.

1 cup water
12 whole cloves
½ cup raisins
1 package (3 oz.) Jell-O Orange or
Orange-Pineapple Gelatin
¾ cup orange juice
1 can (8¾ oz.) crushed pineapple
1 teaspoon grated lemon rind

Bring water, cloves, and raisins to a boil. Remove from heat; discard cloves. Add Jell-O Gelatin and stir until dissolved. Then add orange juice, pineapple, and lemon rind. Pour into individual molds, a 1-quart mold, or an 8x4x3-inch loaf pan. Chill until firm. Unmold on lettuce. Makes about 3 cups, or 6 side salads.

NOTE: For an attractive relish, use juice from 3 oranges, halved, in above recipe; save rinds. To serve, spoon chilled salad into the orange rinds.

CALIFORNIA FRUIT SALAD

The sunshine of the West is reflected in this delightful salad creation.

1 package (3 oz.) Jell-O Lemon or
Orange Gelatin
1 cup boiling water
⅔ cup cold water
½ teaspoon vinegar
2 tablespoons lemon juice
1 orange, sectioned and diced
½ teaspoon grated lemon rind
1 teaspoon grated orange rind
1 tablespoon diced pimiento
⅔ cup diced avocado (optional)

Dissolve Jell-O Gelatin in boiling water. Add cold water, vinegar, and lemon juice. Chill until very thick. Fold in remaining ingredients. Pour into a 1-quart mold or individual molds. Chill until firm. Unmold on salad greens. Garnish with additional avocado, if desired. Makes 3 cups (with avocado), or 6 side salads.

SUNSET SALAD

An appealing, always popular mold of grated carrots and crushed pineapple.

1 package (3 oz.) Jell-O Lemon
 or Orange-Pineapple Gelatin
½ teaspoon salt
1½ cups boiling water
1 can (8¾ oz.) crushed pineapple or pineapple tidbits
1 tablespoon lemon juice
1 cup coarsely grated carrots
⅓ cup chopped pecans (optional)

Dissolve Jell-O Gelatin and salt in boiling water. Add undrained pineapple and lemon juice. Chill until very thick. Then fold in carrots and pecans. Pour into individual molds or a 1-quart mold. Chill until firm. Unmold. Garnish with additional pineapple, if desired. Makes about 3 cups, or 6 side salads.

Barbecue Cubes accent a tossed salad of greens, shrimp, grapefruit.

OLD-FASHIONED COLE SLAW

Creamy cole slaw stays fresh and flavorful in a tangy gelatin mold.

    1 package (3 oz.) Jell-O Orange
        or Orange-Pineapple Gelatin
  ½ teaspoon salt
    1 cup boiling water
    2 tablespoons vinegar
  ½ cup cold water
  ½ cup mayonnaise
  ½ cup sour cream
    1 teaspoon grated onion
    1 tablespoon prepared mustard
    1 teaspoon sugar
    3 cups shredded cabbage
    2 tablespoons pimiento
    1 tablespoon parsley

Dissolve Jell-O Gelatin and salt in boiling water. Add vinegar and cold water; then stir in remaining ingredients, blending well. Chill until slightly thickened. Pour into a 1-quart mold or individual molds. Chill until firm. Unmold. Makes about 4 cups, or 6 to 8 side salads.

BARBECUE SALAD

A tangy tomato salad or aspic that's excellent as a relish or a salad.

    1 package (3 oz.) Jell-O Lemon,
        Orange, or Orange-Pineapple
        Gelatin
    1 cup boiling water
    1 can (8 oz.) tomato sauce
 1½ tablespoons vinegar
  ½ teaspoon salt
    Dash of pepper
    Additional seasonings*

*If desired for extra flavor, add a little onion juice, Worcestershire sauce, tabasco sauce, or prepared horse-radish.

Dissolve Jell-O Gelatin in boiling water. Add remaining ingredients. Pour into individual molds or 3-cup mold. Chill until firm. Unmold on crisp greens. Makes about 2 cups, or 4 side salads or 6 relish servings.

Barbecue Cubes: (Pictured above) Prepare Barbecue Salad, reducing water to ¾ cup. Pour into 8-inch square pan; chill until firm. Cut into cubes and serve on salad greens.

Possible Barbecue Salad additions:
- ¼ cup mayonnaise
- 1 cup cottage cheese
- 1 package (3 oz.) cream cheese, softened
- 1 cup diced celery
- ¼ cup thinly sliced stuffed olives
- 1 cup diced raw or cooked vegetables
- 1 cup diced cooked shrimp
- 1 can (6½ oz.) crab meat, drained
- 1 can (7 oz.) tuna, drained

Shrimp Boat: Prepare Barbecue Salad, doubling all ingredients; pour into a 1½-quart ring mold and chill until firm. Unmold on salad greens and fill center of ring with 1 pound cooked shrimp. Makes about 5 cups gelatin, or 4 or 5 entree servings.

Barbecue Cheese Cracker Pie: Prepare Barbecue Salad; chill until slightly thickened. Meanwhile, mix 1 cup cheese cracker crumbs and ¼ cup melted butter; press firmly on bottom and sides of an 8-inch pie pan. Chill thoroughly. Then pour Barbecue Salad into crust; chill until firm. Serve as appetizer with sea food, if desired. Makes 6 to 8 servings.

NEAPOLITAN SALAD

Three beautiful layers of vegetables are molded in a tangy gelatin mixture.

- 1 package (3 oz.) Jell-O Lemon or Lime Gelatin
- 1 teaspoon salt
- 1 cup boiling water
- ¾ cup cold water
- Dash of pepper
- 2 tablespoons vinegar
- 1 can (1 lb.) whole tomatoes, drained and chopped
- 2 stuffed green olives, sliced
- 1 can (1 lb.) sliced or diced carrots, drained
- 1 can (1 lb.) lima beans, drained

Dissolve Jell-O Gelatin and salt in boiling water. Add cold water, pepper, and vinegar. Arrange tomatoes

and olive slices in bottom of a 1½-quart mold. Add a layer of carrots, then one of lima beans. Pour gelatin gently over vegetables. Chill until firm. Unmold on salad greens. Makes about 6 cups, or 10 to 12 side salads. *NOTE:* If desired, substitute 1 can (12 oz.) whole kernel corn, drained, for the tomatoes or carrots.

CHICKEN SALAD SURPRISE

Cubes of molded chicken salad adorn a tossed green salad.

- 1 package (3 oz.) Jell-O Lemon, Orange, or Orange-Pineapple Gelatin
- 1 teaspoon garlic salt
- ¾ cup boiling water
- 1½ teaspoons grated onion
- Dash of pepper
- 1 tablespoon wine vinegar
- 1 cup sour cream or mayonnaise
- ¼ cup chopped pecans
- 2 cups diced cooked chicken*
- ½ cup diced celery
- 4 quarts torn salad greens
- ⅓ cup sliced ripe olives
- ½ cup drained canned pineapple tidbits
- 2 medium tomatoes, diced

*Or use 1 can (12 oz.) boned chicken, drained and diced.

Dissolve Jell-O Gelatin and garlic salt in boiling water. Add onion, pepper, and vinegar; cool. Blend in sour cream. Chill until very thick. Fold in pecans, chicken, and celery. Pour into 9-inch square pan. Chill until firm. Cut into cubes. Toss remaining ingredients lightly with salad dressing, if desired, and place in salad bowls. Arrange cubes on salads (do not toss). Makes 6 entree servings.

Shrimp Salad Surprise: (Pictured on page 66) Prepare Chicken Salad Surprise, using ¾ cup diced apples and 1½ cups diced cooked shrimp instead of chicken; substitute 1 grapefruit, sectioned, and 1 package (9 oz.) Birds Eye Artichoke Hearts, cooked and drained, for pineapple.

BEET SALAD

An unusual red salad or relish to grace your menu any time of year.

1 can (1 lb.) diced pickled beets
1 package (3 oz.) Jell-O Lemon
   or Lime Gelatin
¾ teaspoon salt
1 cup boiling water
2 teaspoons vinegar
1½ teaspoons prepared horse-
   radish
2 teaspoons grated onion
¾ cup diced celery

Drain beets, measuring liquid; add water to make 1 cup. Dissolve Jell-O Gelatin and salt in boiling water. Add beet liquid, vinegar, horse-radish, and onion. Chill until very thick. Fold in beets and celery. Spoon into individual molds; chill until firm. Unmold. Makes 3½ cups, or 8 relish servings.

COOLIME SALAD

This creamy green salad tastes as cool and delicious as it looks.

1 package (3 oz.) Jell-O Lime
   Gelatin
1 teaspoon salt
¾ cup boiling water
1 cup cottage cheese
1 cup buttermilk
1 tablespoon white vinegar
1 tablespoon prepared horse-
   radish
Dash of pepper
Dash of paprika
1 tablespoon finely chopped onion
½ cup finely chopped celery
¼ cup thin radish slices*

*If desired, omit radish slices and garnish salad with radish roses and cucumber sticks.

Dissolve Jell-O Gelatin and salt in boiling water. Cool to room temperature. Beat the cheese until smooth. Stir buttermilk, vinegar, horse-radish, pepper, paprika, and cheese into gelatin. Chill until very thick. Fold in remaining ingredients. Pour into a 1-quart mold. Chill until firm. Unmold. Makes about 4 cups, or 8 side salads.

RHUBARB SALAD

This new salad is a tangy, crisp contrast to the meat course.

3 cups diced fresh rhubarb
½ cup sugar
¼ teaspoon salt
2 packages (3 oz. each) or
   1 package (6 oz.) Jell-O
   Strawberry Gelatin
2 cups cold water
2 cups finely diced celery
¼ cup lemon juice

Combine rhubarb, sugar, and salt in a saucepan. Cook over low heat until rhubarb is tender. *Do not stir or add water*—rhubarb makes its own juice and pieces should stay whole. Then bring mixture quickly to a boil. Immediately remove from heat and add Jell-O Gelatin, stirring gently just until dissolved. Then add remaining ingredients. Chill until very thick. Spoon into individual molds or a 1½-quart mold. Chill until firm. Unmold. Makes about 5½ cups, or 10 to 12 side salads or about 15 relish servings.

CHEESE VEGETABLE SALAD

A well-seasoned salad of crisp, fresh vegetables and cottage cheese.

1 package (3 oz.) Jell-O Lime or
   Lemon Gelatin
¾ teaspoon salt
1 cup boiling water
¾ cup cold water
1 tablespoon vinegar
1 cup cottage cheese
2 tablespoons diced green pepper
¼ cup diced celery
1 teaspoon grated onion
Dash of pepper
Dash of tabasco sauce

Dissolve Jell-O Gelatin and salt in boiling water. Add cold water and vinegar. Chill until very thick. Then blend in remaining ingredients. Spoon into a 1-quart mold. Chill until firm. Unmold. Makes about 3 cups, or 6 side salads.

VEGETABLE SALAD
(Pictured below)

Your favorite vegetables can be used in this very versatile salad.

1 package (3 oz.) Jell-O Lemon, Lime, Orange, or Orange-Pineapple Gelatin
¾ teaspoon salt
1 cup boiling water
¾ cup cold water
2 tablespoons vinegar
2 teaspoons grated onion
Dash of pepper
¾ cup finely chopped cabbage*
¾ cup finely chopped celery*
¼ cup finely chopped green pepper*
2 tablespoons diced pimiento*

*Or use any vegetable combination listed below or 1 to 2 cups of your favorites.

Dissolve Jell-O Gelatin and salt in boiling water. Add cold water, vinegar, onion, and pepper. Chill until very thick. Then fold in vegetables.

Pour into a 1-quart mold or individual molds. Chill until firm. Unmold. Makes about 3 cups, or 6 side salads or 8 to 10 relish servings.

Other Vegetable Combinations:
Use 1¼ cups cauliflower florets and ¼ cup diced pimiento.
Use ¾ cup diced tomato and ½ cup each diced cucumber and celery.
Use ¾ cup grated carrots and ¼ cup finely chopped green pepper.
Use 1½ cups finely chopped cabbage, ½ cup sliced stuffed olives, and 2 tablespoons chopped parsley.
Use ½ cup each thinly sliced radishes and chopped celery and ¼ cup thin onion rings.

Molded Entree Salad: (Pictured on page 67) Prepare Vegetable Salad using ¼ cup thinly sliced radishes, 1 cup finely shredded lettuce, and ½ cup each slivered cooked ham and swiss cheese instead of the vegetables. Makes 3 entree servings.

Summer Salad (page 52) and a couple versions of Vegetable Salad.

MANDARIN SALAD

An ingenious, refreshing mold of oranges, onion, and celery.

 1 package (3 oz.) Jell-O Orange, Orange-Pineapple, or Lemon Gelatin
 1 cup boiling water
 1 can (11 oz.) mandarin oranges*
 ¼ cup mayonnaise
 ¼ cup thin onion rings
 ½ cup diced celery

*Or use 1 cup drained diced fresh orange sections and ¾ cup cold water.

Dissolve Jell-O Gelatin in boiling water. Drain oranges, measuring syrup. Add water to make ¾ cup; add to gelatin. Blend in mayonnaise. Chill until very thick. Fold in onion, celery, and oranges. Spoon into individual molds or a 1-quart mold. Chill until firm. Unmold. Makes about 3 cups, or 6 side salads or 8 relish servings.

VARIETY SALAD

Using muffin pans as molds and an assortment of salad tidbits, make an array of appetizers or salads.

 1 package (3 oz.) Jell-O Lemon, Lime, or Orange-Pineapple Gelatin
 1½ teaspoons salt
 1 cup boiling water
 1½ teaspoons olive oil
 ½ cup cold water
 2 teaspoons vinegar
 1 small clove garlic, crushed
 Black pepper
 Oregano
 Salad Tidbits*

*Use diced or sliced hard-cooked egg, sliced celery, diced pimiento, diced green pepper, chopped cucumber, cauliflower florets, button or sliced mushrooms, chopped pickle, diced tomato, sliced olives, flaked drained tuna, capers, anchovies, chopped pickled herring, cooked cut green beans, grated carrots, raisins, cubed cheese, or nuts.

Dissolve Jell-O Gelatin and salt in boiling water. Stir in oil, cold water, vinegar, garlic, and a couple dashes *each* pepper and oregano. Place 1 or 2 tablespoons of a Salad Tidbit in each cup of muffin pan. Then fill cups with gelatin. Chill until firm. Unmold on tray or baking sheet. Serve on lettuce as appetizer or salad. Makes 8 to 12 small servings, depending on amount of tidbit in each.

SAVORY SPINACH SALAD

A delicious, dark green salad to highlight meals and delight diners.

 1 package (3 oz.) Jell-O Lemon or Lime Gelatin
 ½ teaspoon salt
 1 cup boiling water
 ½ cup cold water
 3 tablespoons vinegar
 1½ cups chopped cooked spinach
 2 teaspoons grated onion

Dissolve Jell-O Gelatin and salt in boiling water. Add cold water and vinegar. Chill until very thick. Fold in spinach and onion. Pour into a 1-quart mold or individual molds. Chill until firm. Unmold on crisp lettuce. Garnish with mayonnaise and sliced hard-cooked egg, if desired. Makes about 3 cups, or 6 side salads.

PENNY-WISE SALAD

This tasty salad is economical in cost, but there's no shortage of flavor.

 1 package (3 oz.) Jell-O Lemon or Lime Gelatin
 1 teaspoon salt
 1 cup boiling water
 ¾ cup cold water
 2 tablespoons vinegar
 1 tablespoon prepared horse-radish
 ¾ cup finely shredded cabbage
 ¾ cup diced apples

Dissolve Jell-O Gelatin and salt in boiling water. Add cold water, vinegar, and horse-radish. Chill until very thick. Fold in cabbage and apples. Pour into individual molds or a 1-quart mold. Chill until firm. Unmold on crisp greens. Serve with a creamy salad dressing, if desired. Makes about 3½ cups, or 6 side salads.

CHICKEN MOUSSE
(Pictured below)

A hearty flavorful entree for hot summer or busy, meeting-filled days.

- 1 package (3 oz.) Jell-O Lemon
  or Orange-Pineapple Gelatin
- ½ teaspoon salt
- 1¾ cups boiling chicken broth*
  Dash of cayenne
- 2 tablespoons vinegar
- ⅓ cup whipping cream
- ⅓ cup mayonnaise
- 1 cup diced cooked chicken*
- 1 cup finely chopped celery
- 1 tablespoon chopped pimiento

*Or use 1¾ cups boiling water with 2 chicken bouillon cubes and 1 can (6 oz.) boned chicken, drained and diced.

Dissolve Jell-O Gelatin and salt in boiling broth. Add cayenne and vinegar; chill until very thick. Whip the cream. Fold cream and mayonnaise into gelatin, blending well. Then fold in remaining ingredients. Pour into a 1-quart mold or individual molds. Chill until firm. Unmold. Makes 4 cups, or 4 entree servings.

NOTE: For a more decorative salad, pour ¼ cup gelatin into a 1-quart ring mold before adding cream and mayonnaise, arrange additional pimiento in gelatin, and chill until set, but not firm. Then gently spoon Chicken Mousse into mold and chill until firm. Unmold. Fill center of ring with potato salad, if desired.

Ham Mousse: Prepare Chicken Mousse, substituting boiling water for the broth and ground cooked ham for the chicken. Reduce celery to ½ cup and add ½ cup chopped sweet pickles, 1 teaspoon grated onion, and ½ teaspoon Worcestershire sauce.

Salmon Mousse: Prepare Chicken Mousse, using boiling water instead of broth, 1 can (7¾ oz.) flaked salmon instead of chicken, and 1 cup diced cucumber (salted and drained) instead of celery and pimiento.

Tuna Mousse: Prepare Chicken Mousse, using boiling water instead of broth and 1 can (7 oz.) flaked drained tuna instead of chicken.

Chicken Mousse—filled with potato salad, this ring makes a meal.

HAM SALAD DE LUXE

A hearty salad of ham and celery in a well-seasoned gelatin mixture.

**1 package (3 oz.) Jell-O Lemon
  or Orange Gelatin**
½ teaspoon salt
1 cup boiling water
¾ cup cold water
3 tablespoons vinegar
1½ cups finely diced cooked ham
1 cup finely chopped celery
**2 tablespoons finely chopped
  sweet pickle**
½ teaspoon grated onion

Dissolve Jell-O Gelatin and salt in boiling water. Add cold water and vinegar; chill until very thick. Add remaining ingredients. Pour into a 1-quart mold; chill until firm. Unmold. Makes 3⅓ cups, or 3 entree servings.

SOUFFLÉ SALAD

A versatile salad that can contain meat, vegetables, or fruit—serve as a main dish, side salad, or dessert.

**1 package (3 oz.) Jell-O Lemon
  or Lime Gelatin**
¼ teaspoon salt
1 cup boiling water
½ cup cold water
**1 to 2 tablespoons vinegar or
  lemon juice**
¼ cup mayonnaise
Dash of pepper*
1 tablespoon grated onion*
**1½ to 2½ cups raw or cooked
  vegetables***

*Or use 1½ to 2½ cups cooked meat, fish, or poultry; diced cheese or cottage cheese; sliced or chopped hard-cooked eggs; or fresh, canned, or frozen fruit, drained. Omit pepper and onion in fruit salads.

Dissolve Jell-O Gelatin and salt in boiling water. Add cold water, vinegar, mayonnaise, and pepper. Beat to blend well. Pour into shallow pan. Place in freezer 15 to 20 minutes, or until firm about 1 inch around edge and soft in center. Pour into a bowl and whip until fluffy and thick.

Fold in onion and vegetables. Pour into a 1-quart mold or individual molds. Chill until firm—30 to 60 minutes. Unmold on salad greens. Makes about 4 cups, or 4 entree servings or 6 to 8 side salads.

Chicken-Pineapple Soufflé Salad: Prepare Soufflé Salad, omitting pepper and onion, using 1½ cups (12-oz. can) diced cooked chicken instead of vegetables, and adding ½ cup diced celery and 1 can (8¾ oz.) drained crushed pineapple with the chicken.

Garden Soufflé Salad: Prepare Soufflé Salad, using ⅓ cup each diced raw cauliflower, shredded carrots, sliced radishes, diced celery, and chopped watercress and 2 tablespoons diced green pepper for vegetables.

Summer Soufflé Salad: Prepare Soufflé Salad, using lemon juice instead of vinegar, omitting pepper and onion, and using 1 cup diced drained canned peaches, ¾ cup cottage cheese, ½ cup diced celery, and ¼ cup chopped nuts instead of vegetables. Jell-O Orange Gelatin may be substituted for the lemon or lime gelatin.

POLYNESIAN SALAD

A main-dish salad of rice and ham, with an Oriental flavor.

1⅔ cups water
¾ teaspoon salt
⅔ cup Minute Rice
**1 package (3 oz.) Jell-O Orange-
  Pineapple or Orange Gelatin**
1 cup boiling water
1 tablespoon soy sauce
⅓ cup mayonnaise
1 tablespoon vinegar
¾ cup finely chopped ham
½ cup bean sprouts, drained
**2 tablespoons sliced water
  chestnuts**
½ cup finely chopped celery
**1 tablespoon finely chopped
  scallions**
**1 can (1 lb. 14 oz.) sliced pine-
  apple, drained**

Ring-Around-the-Tuna—garnished with curly endive and radish roses.

Bring ⅔ cup water and ¼ teaspoon salt to a boil in saucepan. Stir in rice. Cover, remove from heat, and let stand 5 minutes. Then spread out on tray and chill. Meanwhile, dissolve Jell-O Gelatin in 1 cup boiling water. Add 1 cup water. Chill until very thick. Combine ½ teaspoon salt and remaining ingredients, except pineapple. Then add rice; mix well. Pour 1 cup gelatin into a 1-quart mold. Top with pineapple slices. Add remaining gelatin to rice mixture. Pour into mold. Chill until firm. Unmold on salad greens. Makes about 3½ cups, or 4 entree servings.

RING-AROUND-THE-TUNA
(Pictured above)

A beautiful jewel-like entree salad for your luncheon or buffet table.

1 package (3 oz.) Jell-O Lime or Lemon Gelatin

¼ teaspoon salt
1 cup boiling water
¾ cup cold water
2 tablespoons vinegar
2 teaspoons grated onion
½ cup diced cucumber
½ cup diced celery*
2 tablespoons chopped pimiento*
2 tablespoons sliced stuffed olives
1 can (7 oz.) tuna, drained and flaked

*Or reduce celery to ¼ cup and substitute ½ cup chopped tomato for the pimiento.

Dissolve Jell-O Gelatin and salt in boiling water. Add cold water, vinegar, and onion. Chill until very thick. Stir in remaining ingredients. Pour into individual ring molds or a 1-quart ring mold. Chill until firm. Unmold on crisp salad greens. If desired, serve with additional tuna and top salads with mayonnaise. Makes 3⅔ cups, or about 4 entree servings.

SEA DREAM SALAD

(Pictured on page 50)

Flavorful, green rings to fill with shrimp or a favorite salad.

> 1 package (3 oz.) Jell-O Lime
> Gelatin
> 1¼ cups boiling water
> 1 cup grated cucumber
> 1 tablespoon vinegar
> ¾ teaspoon grated onion
> ½ teaspoon salt
> Dash of cayenne
> 1 pound shrimp, cooked and
> cleaned*

*Or use tuna, salmon, or chicken salad.

Dissolve Jell-O Gelatin in boiling water. Add remaining ingredients, except shrimp; force through sieve. Pour into individual ring molds or a 3-cup or 1-quart ring mold. Chill until firm. Unmold on salad greens. Fill rings with shrimp. Makes 2½ cups gelatin, or 4 entrees with shrimp.

Cheese Dream Salad: Prepare Sea Dream Salad, adding ½ cup cold water; pour only half the gelatin mixture into molds and chill until set, but not firm. Blend remaining gelatin with 1 package (3 oz.) cream cheese, 1 cup diced celery, and ¼ cup sliced green pepper; pour into molds. Chill until firm. Omit shrimp, if desired.

CRAB MEAT SALAD

A deliciously different salad to serve at a luncheon or summer supper.

> 1 package (3 oz.) Jell-O Lemon
> or Lime Gelatin
> ¼ teaspoon salt
> 1 cup boiling water
> ½ cup cold water
> Dash of pepper
> 1 tablespoon lemon juice
> ½ cup cottage cheese
> 1¼ cups (6½-oz. can) crab meat
> ½ cup diced celery
> ¼ cup mayonnaise

Dissolve Jell-O Gelatin and salt in boiling water. Add cold water, pepper, and lemon juice. Chill very

thick. Fold in cottage cheese, crab meat, celery, and mayonnaise. Pour into a 1-quart mold. Chill until firm. Unmold on salad greens. Makes about 4 cups, or 4 entree servings.

De Luxe Crab Salad: Prepare Crab Meat Salad, adding 1 cup whipped cream with the mayonnaise.

CUCUMBER CREAM SALAD

A refreshing salad to serve as individual molds with your meals.

> 1 package (3 oz.) Jell-O Lime
> Gelatin
> 1 teaspoon salt
> 1 cup boiling water
> 2 tablespoons vinegar
> 1 teaspoon grated onion or
> onion juice
> 1 cup sour cream
> ½ cup mayonnaise
> 2 cups drained minced cucumbers

Dissolve Jell-O Gelatin and salt in boiling water. Add vinegar and onion. Chill until very thick. Blend in sour cream and mayonnaise. Then fold in cucumbers. Spoon into individual molds or a 1-quart mold. Chill until firm. Unmold on crisp greens. Makes about 4 cups, or 8 side salads.

Shrimp Salad Surprise (page 59)—
the creamy cubes contain shrimp.

Molded Entree Salad (page 61)—ham and cheese with vegetables.

PARTY POTATO SALAD

*A novel way to make potato salad
more delicious and decorative.*

    2 packages (3 oz. each)
      Jell-O Lemon or Orange-
      Pineapple Gelatin
    Dash of salt
    3 cups boiling water
    ¼ cup vinegar
      Green pepper rings, halved
      Pimiento strips
    3½ cups well-seasoned potato
      salad*
    ¼ cup finely diced cucumber,
      salted and drained
*Use your favorite recipe.

Dissolve Jell-O Gelatin and salt in
boiling water; add vinegar. To ⅔
cup mixture, add 3 tablespoons additional water. Pour into 1½-quart
mold. Chill until slightly thickened.
Arrange green pepper and pimiento
on top. Chill until set, but not firm.

Chill remaining gelatin until very
thick. Whip until fluffy—see directions on page 84. Fold in potato salad
and cucumber. Pour into mold. Chill
until firm. Unmold on lettuce. Makes
about 6 cups, or 10 to 12 side salads.

TOMATO SURPRISE

*A can of flavorful stewed tomatoes
becomes a tempting mold.*

    1 can (1 lb.) stewed tomatoes
    1 package (3 oz.) Jell-O Lemon,
      Strawberry, or Mixed Fruit
      Gelatin
    ½ teaspoon salt
    1 tablespoon vinegar or lemon
      juice

Pour tomatoes into saucepan, saving
can to use as mold. Bring tomatoes to
a boil; add Jell-O Gelatin and salt,
stirring until dissolved. Add vinegar.
Pour into can. Chill until firm. To unmold, puncture bottom of can before
dipping in warm water—see Tips on
Unmolding Jell-O Gelatin on page 82.
Serve with mayonnaise, if desired.
Makes about 2 cups, or 4 side salads
or 6 relish servings.

Tomato Pineapple Surprise: Prepare
Tomato Surprise, increasing vinegar
to 1½ tablespoons and adding 1 can
(8¾ oz.) crushed pineapple, drained,
and ⅛ teaspoon allspice. Pour into
empty tomato and pineapple cans;
chill until firm. Makes about 2½ cups.

MINTED PINEAPPLE

(Pictured below)

Mint-flavored pineapple is a delicious contrast to hearty meats.

- 1 package (3 oz.) Jell-O Lime
  or Lemon Gelatin
  Pinch of salt
- ¾ cup boiling water
- 1 can (1 lb. 4½ oz.) crushed
  pineapple or pineapple tidbits
- 6 drops mint extract
- ½ tablespoon vinegar

Dissolve Jell-O Gelatin and salt in boiling water. Stir in remaining ingredients, saving can to use as mold. Chill until slightly thickened. Pour into the can and 1 individual mold or a serving bowl. Chill until firm. Unmold. (To unmold from can, puncture bottom before dipping in warm water—see Tips on Unmolding Jell-O Gelatin, page 82.) Makes 3¼ cups, or 6 side salads or 10 relish servings.

QUICK TOMATO MOLD

(Pictured below)

For an unusual appetizer, salad, or relish—a tangy tomato juice mixture that's molded in the juice can.

- 1 can (1 pt. 2 oz.) tomato juice
- 1 package (3 oz.) Jell-O Lemon
  or Mixed Fruit Gelatin
- 1½ tablespoons lemon juice
  or vinegar
- ½ teaspoon salt
  Dash of pepper

Bring 1 cup tomato juice to a boil. Stir in Jell-O Gelatin until dissolved. Then pour into juice can, blending with remaining juice. Add seasonings. Chill until firm. To unmold, puncture bottom of can before dipping in warm water -see Tips on Unmolding Jell-O Gelatin on page 82. Slice or serve from a relish dish. Makes 2¾ cups, or 4 to 6 side salads or 8 to 10 relish servings.

Spiced Peaches (page 69), Minted Pineapple, and Quick Tomato Mold— easy relishes or salads that can be molded in fruit cans or molds.

CORN RELISH

A tangy, colorful meat accompaniment you can make with ease.

1 package (3 oz.) Jell-O Lemon
    or Orange Gelatin
1½ teaspoons salt
¾ cup boiling water
1 can (1 lb.) whole kernel corn
½ cup sweet pickle relish
1 tablespoon chopped pimiento

Dissolve Jell-O Gelatin and salt in boiling water. Add remaining ingredients, saving the can to use as a mold. Chill until slightly thickened. Pour into can and 3 individual molds or a 1-quart serving dish. Chill until firm. Unmold. (To unmold relish in can, puncture bottom before dipping in warm water—see Tips on Unmolding Jell-O Gelatin, page 82.) Makes 3¼ cups, or 8 to 10 relish servings.

SPICED PEACHES

(Pictured on opposite page)

A tempting mold that's ever so versatile—serve it as relish or salad.

1 can (1 lb. 1 oz.) sliced cling
    peaches
¼ cup vinegar
½ cup sugar
12 whole cloves
⅛ teaspoon cinnamon
1 package (3 oz.) Jell-O Orange
    or Orange-Pineapple Gelatin
¾ cup cold water

Drain peaches, measuring ¾ cup syrup; save the can to use as mold. Chop peaches coarsely. Bring syrup, vinegar, sugar, and spices slowly to a boil. Add peaches; simmer 10 minutes. Strain syrup and discard cloves. Add boiling water to make 1 cup, if necessary. Dissolve Jell-O Gelatin in hot syrup. Add cold water and peaches. Chill until slightly thickened. Pour into the can and 1 individual mold, or several individual molds or a serving bowl. Chill until firm. Unmold. (To unmold gelatin in can, puncture bottom before dipping in warm water—see Tips on Unmolding Jell-O Gelatin on page 82.) Makes about 2¼ cups, or 4 side salads or 6 to 8 relish servings.

To use fresh peaches: Prepare Spiced Peaches, using 3 fresh peaches, peeled and sliced, instead of canned peaches and substituting ¾ cup water for the peach syrup.

To use canned apricots: Prepare Spiced Peaches, using 1 can (1 lb. 1 oz.) canned apricot halves instead of the canned peaches.

MOLDED CHEF'S SALAD

The hearty combination of a chef's salad bowl "wrapped up" in tangy gelatin.

1 can (7 oz.) tuna, drained and
    coarsely flaked
1 small tomato, diced and
    drained
2 tablespoons sliced ripe olives
2 tablespoons green pepper strips
2 tablespoons red onion strips
2 tablespoons Italian salad
    dressing
1 package (3 oz.) Jell-O Lemon
    or Lime Gelatin
1 teaspoon salt
1 cup boiling water
¾ cup cold water
2 teaspoons vinegar
1 hard-cooked egg, diced
1½ cups coarsely chopped lettuce
    Creamy Anchovy Dressing

Combine tuna, vegetables, and salad dressing in a bowl. Mix lightly; let stand while preparing gelatin mixture. Dissolve Jell-O Gelatin and salt in boiling water. Add cold water and vinegar. Cool. Pour half into a 5-cup ring mold and add tuna mixture and egg. Top with lettuce. Add remaining gelatin. Cover; chill until firm. Unmold; serve with anchovy dressing. Makes 4 cups, or 4 entree servings.

Creamy Anchovy Dressing: Combine ½ cup mayonnaise, 2 tablespoons cream or milk, and 2 finely chopped anchovy fillets; mix well.

CRANBERRY SURPRISE

Canned cranberry sauce goes from the can into a quick gelatin mold.

1 package (3 oz.) Jell-O Orange, Orange-Pineapple, or Mixed Fruit Gelatin
¾ cup boiling water
1 orange
1 can (7 oz.) whole cranberry sauce

Dissolve Jell-O Gelatin in boiling water. Remove seeds from orange and put through food chopper. Fold cranberry sauce and orange into gelatin, saving can to use as mold. Pour into the can and several individual molds or a serving dish. Chill until firm. Unmold. (To unmold mixture in can, puncture bottom before dipping in warm water—see Tips on Unmolding Jell-O Gelatin on page 82.) Makes about 2½ cups, or 4 side salads or 6 to 8 relish servings.

Fruit Surprise: Prepare Cranberry Surprise, using 1 can (8¾ oz.) drained fruit cocktail instead of orange and chilling gelatin mixture until very thick before adding fruit cocktail.

Marshmallow Surprise: Prepare Cranberry Surprise, using ⅓ cup orange juice and 2 teaspoons grated orange rind instead of entire orange. Chill mixture until very thick; add 1 cup miniature or diced marshmallows.

PARTY CHICKEN SALAD

Crushed pineapple and the crunch of diced celery and pecans give chicken salad an unusually elegant flair.

1 package (3 oz.) Jell-O Lemon or Orange-Pineapple Gelatin
½ teaspoon salt*
1¾ cups boiling chicken consommé*
Dash of pepper
Dash of paprika
2 tablespoons vinegar
¼ cup mayonnaise
1½ cups diced cooked chicken*
½ cup finely diced celery

1 tablespoon chopped pimiento
1 tablespoon chopped parsley
¼ cup drained canned crushed pineapple
¼ cup coarsely chopped pecans
2 tablespoons sweet pickle relish

*Or omit salt and use 2 chicken bouillon cubes in 1¾ cups boiling water and 1 can (12 oz.) boned chicken, drained and diced.

Dissolve Jell-O Gelatin and salt in boiling consommé. Add pepper, paprika, vinegar, and mayonnaise; blend well. Chill until very thick. Then fold in remaining ingredients. Pour into a 1-quart mold. Chill until firm. Unmold on crisp lettuce. Makes about 4 cups, or 4 entree servings.

TUNA SALAD

Tuna at its best — in a well-seasoned salad that stays fresh until served.

1 package (3 oz.) Jell-O Lemon Gelatin
¼ teaspoon salt
1 cup boiling water
½ cup cold water
1 tablespoon lemon juice
½ cup mayonnaise
1 teaspoon grated onion
1 cup chopped cucumber
1 can (7 oz.) tuna, drained and flaked
¼ cup sliced stuffed olives
¼ cup diced celery

Dissolve Jell-O Gelatin and salt in boiling water. Blend in cold water, lemon juice, mayonnaise, and onion; beat to blend well. Chill until very thick. Fold in remaining ingredients. Pour into a 1-quart mold or serving bowl. Chill until firm. Unmold on crisp greens. Serve with more mayonnaise, if desired. Makes about 4 cups or 4 entree servings.

De Luxe Tuna Salad. (Pictured on opposite page) Prepare Tuna Salad, omitting onion, cucumber, and olives and adding ½ cup <u>each</u> cooked peas <u>and</u> chopped apples.

CRANBERRY ORANGE SALAD

A classic salad or relish—especially good with roast turkey and chicken.

- **1 package (3 oz.) Jell-O Orange, Lemon, or Strawberry Gelatin**
- **1 cup boiling water**
- **¾ cup cold water**
- **½ small orange, unpeeled**
- **2 cups fresh cranberries**
- **⅓ cup sugar**

Dissolve Jell-O Gelatin in boiling water. Add cold water. Chill until very thick. Cut orange in wedges and remove seeds. Put orange and cranberries through food chopper. Mix fruit and sugar. Fold into gelatin. Pour into individual molds or a 1-quart mold. Chill until firm. Unmold on crisp lettuce. Makes about 3½ cups, or 6 side salads or 10 relish servings.

CRANBERRY SAUCE

A smooth, tangy relish-type jelly to serve with meats and poultry.

- **2½ cups fresh cranberries**
- **1⅔ cups water**
- **1 package (3 oz.) Jell-O Orange or Lemon Gelatin**
- **⅔ cup sugar**
- **Dash of salt**

Cook cranberries in water until skins pop. Drain, measuring juice. Add boiling water to make 1½ cups. Dissolve Jell-O Gelatin, sugar, and salt in hot liquid. Press cranberries through sieve and add sieved pulp to gelatin. Pour into a 1-quart mold or individual molds. Chill until firm. Unmold. Garnish with mint and serve with mayonnaise, if desired. Makes about 2 cups, or 6 relish servings.

De Luxe Tuna Salad (page 70)—mayonnaise makes the salad creamy.

MARZIPAN

MARZIPAN
(Pictured on opposite page)

Easy-to-make confections that look just like those you've seen in pictures.

> 1 package (7 oz.) Baker's Cookie Coconut
> 1 package (3 oz.) Jell-O Gelatin (any fruit flavor)
> 1 cup grated blanched almonds
> 2/3 cup sweetened condensed milk
> 1½ teaspoons sugar
> 1 teaspoon almond extract

Thoroughly mix all ingredients. Shape as small fruits, vegetables, hearts, Easter eggs, or other forms. If desired, use food coloring to paint details on fruit and add stems of whole cloves or angelica. Chill until dry. Store, covered, at room temperature. Makes 2 to 3 dozen candies.

NOTE: For fruits, use the appropriate flavors: Jell-O Strawberry Gelatin for strawberries; Jell-O Lemon Gelatin for bananas, lemons, pears; Jell-O Lime Gelatin for "green" apples; Jell-O Lime Gelatin for leaves, limes; Jell-O Orange Gelatin for oranges; Jell-O Cherry or Black Cherry Gelatin for cherries.

CRANBERRY ICE

A smooth, slightly tart frozen treat that's excellent as appetizer or relish.

> 1 pound fresh cranberries
> 5 cups water
> 1 cup sugar
> 1 package (3 oz.) Jell-O Lemon or Mixed Fruit Gelatin

Cook cranberries in the water until skins burst. Mash berries with fork; strain through coarse sieve. Heat strained sauce; add sugar and blend well. Remove from heat and stir in Jell-O Gelatin until dissolved. Pour into shallow pans; cool to room temperature. Freeze 2 hours, or until almost firm. Spoon into a chilled bowl; beat until fluffy. Return to pans; freeze until firm—2 to 3 hours. Makes about 2 quarts, or 12 servings.

New Ways

With Jell-O Gelatin

Neither years nor constant use lessens Jell-O Gelatin's variety. There are always new ways to use it. For instance, sprinkle Jell-O right out of the package over frosted cakes or on baked cookies that have been brushed with corn syrup. And try out the appetizers, glazed meats and sandwiches, dessert toppings, and candies—all things you keep meaning to have a go at but never do. Go on now, you seem to have a little time.

CONTINENTAL CHEESE MOLD

An elegant cheese mixture to serve with crackers or fresh vegetables.

1 package (3 oz.) Jell-O Lemon
　　or Lime Gelatin
¾ cup boiling water
½ cup sour cream
2½ cups creamed cottage cheese
4 ounces Roquefort or bleu
　　cheese, crumbled
2½ teaspoons seasoned salt
¾ teaspoon Worcestershire sauce
½ teaspoon lemon juice
2 tablespoons minced chives

Dissolve Jell-O Gelatin in boiling water; chill until very thick. Meanwhile, combine remaining ingredients, except chives; beat until smooth. Then add gelatin, blending well. Fold in chives. Pour into a 1-quart mold. Chill until firm. Unmold; serve as appetizer with assorted crackers and fresh vegetables. Makes about 4 cups.

DANISH FRUIT SOUP

A sensational, tart-sweet red raspberry appetizer or dessert.

1 package (3 oz.) Jell-O Rasp-
　　berry or Mixed Fruit Gelatin
Dash of salt
1 cup boiling water
1 package (10 oz.) Birds Eye
　　Red Raspberries
1 tablespoon lemon juice
1½ cups cold water*
½ cup sour cream
Nutmeg

*For a thinner soup, increase the cold water to 2 cups.

Dissolve Jell-O Gelatin and salt in boiling water. Add the frozen raspberries, stirring until berries separate. Then stir in lemon juice and cold water. Chill 30 to 40 minutes. Season the sour cream with nutmeg to taste, and serve on soup. Makes about 3½ cups, or 6 to 8 servings.

Creamy Fruit Soup: Prepare Danish Fruit Soup, stirring sour cream into soup. Sprinkle soup with nutmeg.

BLEU CHEESE DE LUXE MOLD

This mold is delicious as spread for crackers or apple wedges or as salad.

1 package (3 oz.) Jell-O Lemon
　　Gelatin
1 cup boiling water
¼ cup cold water
¼ cup dry white wine
½ cup sour cream
½ cup crumbled bleu cheese
2 cups finely diced unpeeled red
　　apples (optional)

Dissolve Jell-O Gelatin in boiling water. Add cold water and wine. Then blend in sour cream. Chill until very thick. Stir in cheese and apples. Pour into a 1-quart mold or individual molds. Chill until firm. Unmold on lettuce and serve with crackers or apple wedges. Makes about 2½ cups without apples or 4 cups with apples, or 6 to 8 side salads.

GLAZED APPLES

Top-of-the-stove "baked" apples with a shiny, sweet glaze.

1 package (3 oz.) each Jell-O
　　Strawberry-Banana and
　　Orange Gelatins
1½ cups boiling water
1 cup cold water
6 large red baking apples
1 large stick cinnamon
6 whole cloves

Dissolve Jell-O Gelatins in 1½ cups boiling water. Add 1 cup cold water. Core apples and pare off a 1-inch strip of skin at stem end of each. Place apples, stem end up, in a large skillet.

Pour gelatin over apples; add spices. Bring to a boil over medium heat. Cover, reduce heat, and simmer 15 minutes, or until tender. Then uncover and place under broiler, about 2 inches from heat, basting frequently for 15 minutes, or until apples are glazed and lightly browned. Serve warm with syrup. Or chill apples and syrup separately; then flake or cube the set syrup and serve with the apples. Makes 6 servings.

Glazed Apple Rings: Prepare Glazed Apples, using 3 large red apples instead of 6. Core the apples, but do not remove skin. Slice into rings about ½ inch thick. Place in skillet with gelatin mixture and spices. Cover and simmer 5 minutes, or until tender; then broil, basting frequently, 10 minutes. Use as a garnish for meat, fish, or poultry.

CHERRY-GLAZED HAM

An ever-so-simple, beautiful red glaze that makes a ham festive.

**1 smoked picnic ham
Whole cloves
1 package (3 oz.) Jell-O Cherry
   Gelatin
½ cup firmly packed brown sugar
1 cup boiling water**

Bake ham according to directions given on wrapper, removing ham from oven about 45 minutes before baking period is finished. Remove rind, score fat, and garnish with whole cloves. Dissolve Jell-O Gelatin and sugar in boiling water. Pour about a third of the mixture over ham and return to oven. Allow to bake remaining 45 minutes, basting frequently with remaining gelatin mixture.

To serve hot, slice ham and serve, using drippings in pan for sauce. To serve cold, place ham on serving platter and cool; then chill for several hours. Meanwhile, pour drippings into a cup or bowl and let stand a few minutes; then skim off fat. Pour remainder into a shallow pan. Chill until firm. Just before serving, flake or cube and place around ham.

NOTE: To glaze a large smoked ham, use 1 package (6 oz.) Jell-O Cherry Gelatin, 1 cup firmly packed brown sugar, and 2 cups boiling water.

Glazed Ham Slice: Prepare glaze as directed for Cherry-Glazed Ham. Place a 1½-inch thick ham slice in shallow baking dish, stick a few whole cloves in ham, and pour on ½ cup glaze. Cover and bake in moderate oven (325°F.) 30 minutes. Then uncover and bake 30 minutes, basting frequently with remaining glaze.

HERB-GLAZED SANDWICHES

Your luncheon or tea sandwiches stay fresh and flavorful under a glaze.

**1⅔ cups water
⅛ teaspoon peppercorns
½ bay leaf
½ teaspoon dried dill
1 package (3 oz.) Jell-O Lemon
   Gelatin
½ teaspoon salt
Dash of cayenne
3 tablespoons vinegar
6 to 8 open-faced sandwiches***

*Or 12 to 14 appetizer-size sandwiches.

Combine water, peppercorns, bay leaf, and dried dill in a saucepan. Cover and simmer about 10 minutes; strain. Dissolve Jell-O Gelatin, salt, and cayenne in the hot liquid. Add vinegar. Chill until syrupy.

Place sandwiches on a rack and pour syrupy gelatin over them, allowing about ¼ cup for each large sandwich or 2 tablespoons for each small sandwich. Chill until glaze is firm. Makes about 1¾ cups glaze.

Sandwich Suggestions:
Pumpernickel bread spread with mustard and topped with swiss cheese, sauerkraut, and corned beef.
Whole wheat bread topped with sliced hard-cooked egg and cooked cleaned shrimp.
Buttered rye bread spread lightly with prepared horse-radish and topped with sliced roast beef and tomato.
Buttered whole wheat bread spread with bleu cheese and topped with sliced chicken and crisp bacon.
Buttered white bread topped with tuna salad and sliced cheese.
Buttered salty rye bread spread with liver pâté and sprinkled with chopped hard-cooked egg.

GLAZED SWEET POTATOES

An easy way to prepare delicious "candied" sweet potatoes.

1 package (3 oz.) Jell-O Orange Gelatin
1/4 cup firmly packed light brown sugar
Dash of salt
1 cup boiling water
1 tablespoon butter
1 can (1 lb.) sweet potatoes, sliced or quartered*

*Or use 6 to 8 cooked sweet potatoes.

Dissolve Jell-O Gelatin, sugar, and salt in boiling water in skillet. Add butter and bring to a boil, stirring constantly. Add sweet potatoes; cook over medium heat about 15 minutes, basting frequently. When syrup thickens and is glossy, remove from heat. Serve hot. Makes 3 to 4 servings.

ORANGE-GLAZED DUCK

A glistening, easy orange glaze for golden roasted duck.

4- or 5-lb. oven-ready duck
Salt
Celery stalks
1 cup water
8 whole cloves
1 package (3 oz.) Jell-O Orange Gelatin
2/3 cup firmly packed brown sugar
1 teaspoon vinegar

Rub duck inside and out with salt. Then pin skin at neck over back of duck. Place celery in body cavity; draw opening together with poultry pins and lace twine around pins. Prick thoroughly with a fork. Place breast side up on rack in a shallow pan. Insert meat thermometer in thigh muscle next to body. Roast in a slow oven (325°F.) 35 to 40 minutes per pound, or to 185°F. on thermometer.

Meanwhile, bring water and cloves to a boil. Remove from heat; stir in Jell-O Gelatin and sugar until dissolved. Add vinegar. About 45 minutes before duck is finished roasting,

pour drippings from pan. Then pour 1/3 cup gelatin over duck. Finish roasting, basting frequently with remaining gelatin. Makes 4 servings.

FROSTED GRAPES

A lovely garnish for salads, meat platters, and desserts—or serve them as delicious desserts.

2 pounds seedless grapes
1 egg white, slightly beaten
1 package (3 oz.) Jell-O Gelatin (any fruit flavor)

Dip small clusters of grapes, one at a time, into beaten egg white and allow excess to drain off. Then sprinkle with Jell-O Gelatin. Chill until dry, about 3 hours. Use as garnish or dessert.

NOTE: If desired, frosted grapes may be stored in refrigerator overnight.

EASTER EGGS

Colorful "eggs" to serve in a nest of green coconut on Easter or to use as garnish around salads all year

1 package (3 oz.) Jell-O Gelatin (any fruit flavor)
1 cup boiling water
1/2 cup cold water
8 egg shells*

*To remove yolks and whites, crack small end of each uncooked egg slightly. Pick away enough shell so that yolk and white will drop out. Rinse inside of shell with cold water. Or pick a small hole in end of egg shell and prick a tiny hole with pin in opposite end; then blow out yolk and white. After rinsing shell, cover tiny hole with tape.

Dissolve Jell-O Gelatin in boiling water. Add cold water. Place egg shells in egg carton. Pour gelatin into shells, using funnel or small pitcher. Chill overnight. Crack shells slightly, dip quickly in warm water, and peel off. Serve in nests of shredded lettuce or green Tinted Coconut (page 78), or use as garnish around potato and other salads. Makes 8 eggs.

NOTE: Use egg yolks and whites in scrambled eggs for Easter breakfast.

Fresh Strawberry Glaze, on cheesecake and cream pie, and Quick Fruit Dessert (page 7)—similar, tasty Jell-O Gelatin and fruit mixtures.

STRAWBERRY GLAZE
(Pictured above)

A luscious, beautiful glaze for pies, cheesecakes, and other desserts.

- 1 package (3 oz.) Jell-O Strawberry Gelatin
- 1 cup boiling water
- 1 package (10 oz.) Birds Eye Strawberries

Dissolve Jell-O Gelatin in boiling water. Add frozen strawberries and stir until berries separate and mixture thickens. Spoon over top of cooled highly fluted 9-inch cream pie or a 9- or 10-inch cheesecake. Chill until firm. Makes 2¼ cups glaze.

Fresh Strawberry Glaze. Prepare Strawberry Glaze, adding ¾ cup cold water instead of frozen berries; chill mixture until slightly thickened. Then add 1 cup sweetened sliced fresh strawberries; spoon over pie. (For 10-inch pie, 1½ cups berries may be used.) Makes about 2½ cups.

FIG-BERRY PRESERVES

The color and flavor of strawberry gelatin is added to fig preserves with this easy-to-make recipe.

- 3 cups mashed figs (about 20 medium figs)*
- 2 packages (3 oz. each) or 1 package (6 oz.) Jell-O Strawberry Gelatin
- 3 cups sugar

*If dark figs are used, preserves will be a deep purple color. For lighter preserves, figs may be peeled.

Thoroughly mix figs, Jell-O Gelatin, and sugar in a *large* saucepan. Bring to a boil over medium heat and continue boiling for 3 minutes, stirring occasionally. Pour quickly into glasses. Cover at once with ⅛ inch hot paraffin. Makes about 6 medium glasses.

NOTE: This recipe may be halved to fill about 3 medium glasses—use 1½ cups mashed figs, 1 package (3 oz.) Jell-O Gelatin, and 1½ cups sugar.

SEVEN MINUTE FROSTING

Gelatin flavors and colors a fluffy frosting with no extra work for you.

2 egg whites, unbeaten
1¼ cups sugar
1 package (3 oz.) Jell-O Gelatin
   (any fruit flavor)
Dash of salt
½ cup water
2 teaspoons light corn syrup

Combine all ingredients in top of double boiler. Beat about 1 minute or until thoroughly mixed. Beat over gently boiling water at high speed of electric mixer or with rotary beater 7 minutes, or until frosting will stand in stiff peaks. (Stir frosting up from bottom and sides of pan occasionally.) Remove from boiling water and spread on cake immediately. Makes about 7 cups, or enough to frost tops and sides of three 8-inch layers (generously), three 9-inch layers, two 10-inch tube cakes, or about 30 cupcakes or the tops only of about 5 to 6 dozen cupcakes.

DIVINITY PASTELS

Lovely candies, that are flavored and colored with fruit flavor gelatin.

3 cups sugar
¾ cup light corn syrup
¾ cup water
2 egg whites
1 package (3 oz.) Jell-O Gelatin
   (any fruit flavor)
1 cup chopped nuts
1 cup Baker's Cookie Coconut
   (optional)

Mix sugar, corn syrup, and water; bring to a boil over low heat, stirring to dissolve sugar. Continue boiling, stirring occasionally, until a little syrup forms a hard ball in cold water (or to 252°F. on a candy thermometer)—about 15 minutes. Meanwhile, beat egg whites until stiff but not dry. Then add Jell-O Gelatin, 1 tablespoon at a time, and beat until mixture will stand in stiff peaks.

Then pour syrup in a thin stream over the egg white mixture, beating constantly. Continue beating until mixture will hold its shape and loses its gloss—about 10 minutes with electric mixer. Add nuts; quickly pour into a well-greased 9-inch square pan, or drop by teaspoonfuls onto wax paper and allow to dry. Let stand in pan until firm enough to handle—about 10 minutes. Cut into 8 strips, roll in coconut, and cut each strip into 10 to 12 pieces. Roll in coconut again. Allow to dry about 2 hours. Store in a covered container. Makes about 7 dozen candies.

NOTE: If candy becomes too stiff during beating, add few drops hot water.

PARTY TOPPING

A flavorful, pastel topping—use as you would whipped cream.

3½ tablespoons (half of a 3-oz.
   package) Jell-O Gelatin
   (any fruit flavor)
⅓ cup boiling water
2 egg whites
¼ cup sugar

Dissolve Jell-O Gelatin in boiling water. Chill until slightly thickened. Beat egg whites until foamy throughout; gradually add sugar and beat until stiff peaks will form. Then gradually add gelatin, beating until well blended. Serve on cake, puddings, and other desserts. Makes 3 cups.

TINTED COCONUT

Flavorful as well as colorful coconut to use as a garnish on desserts.

2 tablespoons Jell-O Gelatin
   (any fruit flavor)
1⅓ cups (about) Baker's Angel
   Flake Coconut

Measure Jell-O Gelatin right from package and combine with coconut in a 1-quart jar. Cover and shake vigorously until coconut is evenly tinted, about 1 minute. Use on frostings, cookies, puddings, and other desserts. Makes 1⅓ cups.

NOTE: Dissolve remaining Jell-O Gelatin in 1 cup hot water. Add ½ cup cold water. Chill until firm—about 3 hours. Makes 1½ cups, or 3 servings.

PASTEL MARSHMALLOWS

Tender, light confections you can use as you would those you buy.

1 package (3 oz.) Jell-O Gelatin (any fruit flavor)
⅔ cup boiling water
1 cup sugar
3 tablespoons light corn syrup
Confectioners' sugar

Dissolve Jell-O Gelatin in boiling water in a saucepan over low heat. Stir in sugar until dissolved. (Do not boil.) Blend in corn syrup. Chill until slightly thickened. Line an 8-inch square pan with wax paper; grease with butter or margarine. Then beat gelatin mixture at highest speed of electric mixer until soft peaks will form, about 5 minutes. Pour into pan. Let stand in refrigerator overnight.

Then place mixture on board heavily dusted with confectioners' sugar. To remove wax paper, dampen surface and let stand a few minutes; then peel off paper. Dust top with sugar. Cut into 1-inch squares. Roll cut edges in sugar. Makes about 6 dozen.

POPCORN BALLS

Colorful popcorn balls are sure to thrill the youngsters when served as party- or snack-time surprises.

1 cup light corn syrup
½ cup sugar
1 package (3 oz.) Jell-O Gelatin (any fruit flavor)
½ pound salted peanuts, coarsely chopped
9 cups popped popcorn

Bring syrup and sugar to a boil. Remove from heat and add Jell-O Gelatin, stirring until dissolved. Add peanuts and pour over popcorn, mixing well. Quickly form into 1½-inch balls. Makes about 4 dozen.

FROZEN POPS
(Pictured below)

Here's an easy-to-make version of the popular frozen treat all children enjoy.

1 package (3 oz.) Jell-O Gelatin (any fruit flavor)
1 envelope Kool-Aid Instant Soft Drink Mix (any flavor)
1 cup sugar
2 cups boiling water
2 cups cold water

Dissolve Jell-O Gelatin, instant soft drink mix, and sugar in boiling water. Add cold water. Pour into ice cube trays, small paper cups, or frozen pop molds. Insert wooden sticks or paper spoons diagonally in each ice cube section or at an angle in molds or cups for handles. (If desired, pops may be partially frozen before handles are inserted.) Freeze until firm—2 to 3 hours. Makes 20 to 24 pops.

Double Orange Pops: Dissolve 1 package (3 oz.) Jell-O Orange Gelatin and ½ cup sugar in 2 cups boiling water. Add 2 cups orange juice. Then freeze pops as directed above.

Frozen Pops—frozen homemade treats the children will enjoy.

(clockwise from bottom)
CUT-OUT (page 86)
CANDY STRIPE PARFAIT (page 86)
TILT-TOP DESSERT (page 86)
WHIPPED JELL-O GELATIN (page 84)
FLAKED JELL-O GELATIN (page 85)
CUBED JELL-O GELATIN (page 85)
(center)
SCALLOPED DESSERT (page 86)

Some tricks used by the experts to make gelatin molds more beautiful.

To prepare Jell-O Gelatin, dissolve the gelatin *completely* in boiling water or other liquid—for a clear, uniformly set mold, gelatin *must* be completely dissolved. Then add cold liquid—or use several ice cubes, see Speed-Set Jell-O Gelatin (page 82).

To double a recipe, use two 3-oz. packages or one 6-oz. package of Jell-O Gelatin and twice the amounts of the other ingredients except salt, vinegar, and lemon juice—you'll find about 1½ times the amounts of these ingredients are sufficient.

For large molds, decrease the required liquid about ¼ cup for each 3 ounces of Jell-O Gelatin. (This has already been done in many recipes in this book for your convenience.) A firmer consistency makes mold less fragile, less likely to crack.

For soft-set Jell-O Gelatin, increase liquid about ½ cup for each 3 ounces of Jell-O Gelatin—this is too soft to unmold, but has excellent eating quality.

To add fruits and vegetables, chill the gelatin until very thick, not set, before adding other ingredients. If gelatin isn't thick enough, fruits and vegetables may float or sink. (Do not add fresh or frozen pineapple, figs, mangoes, or papayas or frozen fruit juice blends containing these fruits—an enzyme in these fruits, when fresh, keeps Jell-O Gelatin from setting. When cooked or canned, these fruits are excellent in Jell-O.)

To mold Jell-O Gelatin, pour it into molds or serving dishes—a 3-oz. package without fruits or vegetables makes 2 cups, a 6-oz. package makes 4 cups. Chill until firm—see chart on page 88. (Any metal pan, bowl, cup, or can may be used as a mold.)

To layer gelatin mixtures, chill each layer until set, but not firm, before

Tips and Tricks

For molding, flaking, and cubing

Jell-O Gelatin is really kid stuff to prepare. However, we have some things for you to do with it that are distinctly adult. Do you know, for example, that you can flake Jell-O, cube it, whip it, layer it, scallop it, and crown it, as well as turn it out in glorious molds? Well, you can. All these things you can do with Jell-O change it somewhat. Oh, it's still delicious, still light, still filled with fresh fruit taste—but somehow it seems a little more exotic. How about it?

adding the next layer—if the first layer is too firm, the layers may slip apart when unmolded. Many layers may be built up in this way. Except for the first layer, the gelatin mixtures should be cool and slightly thickened before being poured into mold—if mixture is warm, it may soften the layer beneath and mixtures may run or mix together.

To make special designs, foods can be arranged in gelatin to make a simple mold more decorative in two ways:

Simple way: Chill gelatin until thick; then pour about ¼ inch gelatin into mold. Place a design of fruits or vegetables in gelatin. Chill until set, but not firm. Then pour remaining cooled gelatin into mold.

Expert way: Pour about ⅛ inch of gelatin into mold; chill until set, but not firm. Cool remaining gelatin. Arrange design on set gelatin, cover carefully with a few spoonfuls cooled gelatin to anchor design, and chill until set, but not firm. Then pour remaining cooled gelatin into the mold.

To chill gelatin molds, leave mold in refrigerator until firm (see chart on page 88). Since metal chills more quickly than glass, gelatin in metal molds will be firm in less time than gelatin in a glass mixing bowl or serving dish. To hasten chilling, chill the mold a few minutes in a pan of ice and water before placing in refrigerator. For storage overnight or longer, it's wise to cover the gelatin to prevent evaporation and drying.

To make one serving, dissolve 1¾ tablespoons Jell-O Gelatin in ½ cup boiling water. Chill until firm.

SPEED-SET JELL-O GELATIN

An easy trick—substitute ice cubes for cold water in preparing gelatin to shorten the required chilling time.

To use ice cubes, dissolve Jell-O Gelatin in boiling water as directed on package; then add ½ tray ice cubes (7 to 10, depending on size) for 3-oz. package Jell-O Gelatin or 14 to 20 ice cubes for 6-oz. package Jell-O Gelatin. Stir about 3 minutes to melt ice, or until gelatin is thickened. Remove any unmelted ice. Pour into serving dishes or individual molds. Chill until soft-set and ready to eat from dishes, about 30 minutes, or until firm enough to unmold, about 1 hour.

To use ice and water mixture, dissolve Jell-O Gelatin in boiling water as directed on package; then substitute a mixture of ice cubes or crushed ice and water for the cold water, stirring until ice melts completely. Chill.

To add fruits or vegetables or to whip, let gelatin stand 5 or 6 minutes to thicken after removing unmelted ice. Then fold in ingredients or whip (see directions on page 84). Chill until firm.

To use premeasured frozen mold, freeze ¾ cup water in a 2- or 3-cup mold for 3-oz. package Jell-O Gelatin or 1½ cups water in a 1-quart mold for 6-oz. package Jell-O Gelatin. Then dissolve Jell-O Gelatin in boiling water as directed on package and pour the hot mixture over ice in mold. Stir until ice is dissolved, or until gelatin starts to thicken. If ice does not melt completely, remove unmelted pieces before chilling mold. To add fruits or vegetables, freeze water in a larger mold to allow space for added ingredients and allow gelatin to stand 3 to 4 minutes to thicken before folding in the ingredients. Chill until firm.

TIPS ON UNMOLDING JELL-O GELATIN

The art of unmolding gelatin is easy to learn—it just takes a little practice.

Before unmolding gelatin, make certain that gelatin is completely firm—it should not feel sticky on top and should not sag toward side if mold is tilted. If gelatin is firm, dip a small pointed knife in warm water and run tip of it around top edge of mold to loosen. Or moisten tips of fingers and

(a) Before unmolding gelatin, run knife tip around top.

(b) Or pull from edge of mold gently with moist fingers.

(c) Dip mold just to rim in warm water for 10 seconds.

(d) Lift from water and shake gently to loosen gelatin.

gently pull gelatin from top edge of mold. When using disposable metal cans as molds, puncture bottoms—this makes it easier to unmold the gelatin because it eliminates any vacuum in cans, which are usually deeper in relationship to top surface than other molds.

Moisten top of gelatin and a chilled plate—the moist surfaces make it easier to slide the gelatin into the center of the plate after it has been unmolded.

Dip mold in warm water—do not use hot water as it will melt the gelatin. (If oven-proof glass, china, or paper containers are used as molds, the water should be slightly warmer.) Working quickly, dip the mold just to the rim in the warm water—about 10 seconds. Lift from water, hold upright, and shake slightly to loosen the gelatin from mold.

Invert moistened plate on mold. Always unmold gelatin on a chilled or

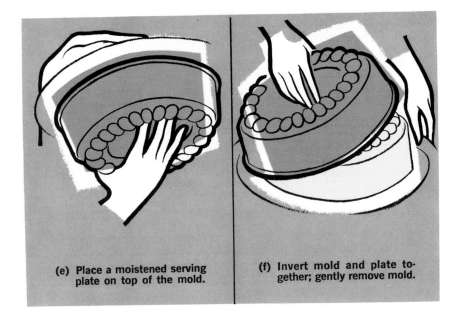

(e) Place a moistened serving plate on top of the mold.

(f) Invert mold and plate together; gently remove mold.

cold plate or platter—a warm plate will melt the gelatin.

Then invert plate and mold together. Lift off mold carefully—if gelatin doesn't release easily, dip the mold in warm water again. If necessary, move gelatin to center of plate.

NOTE: If desired, try this new way of unmolding gelatin. Oil mold slightly; then place a 1-inch strip of aluminum foil across bottom and up sides, letting it extend as tabs on both sides. Smooth foil to remove wrinkles and press to shape of mold. Add gelatin and chill until firm. Then moisten top of gelatin and a plate, place plate over gelatin, and invert together. Gently pull one of the tabs to break vacuum in mold; then remove mold and the foil strip.

HOW TO WHIP JELL-O GELATIN
(Pictured on page 80)

One of the easiest things you can do to change the texture and appearance of Jell-O Gelatin—just whip it until thick and fluffy.

Prepare Jell-O Gelatin (any fruit flavor) as directed on package and chill until very thick. Then beat with rotary beater or electric mixer until mixture is fluffy and thick—about double in volume results in the best eating quality and flavor.

To shorten the chilling and beating times, chill the gelatin until slightly thickened. Then place the bowl of gelatin in another bowl of ice and water before starting to beat.

Pour whipped gelatin into molds or shallow pan, or add cubes of Jell-O Gelatin (page 85) or fruit and pour into molds. Chill until firm. Unmold, cut in squares, or spoon into serving dishes; serve with fruit or a custard sauce, if desired. A 3-oz. package makes about 4 cups, or 4 or 5 servings; a 6-oz. package makes about 8 cups, or 8 to 10 servings.

Snows: Prepare whipped Jell-O Gelatin, adding unbeaten egg whites to the thickened gelatin before starting to beat. Use 1 or 2 egg whites for a 3-oz. package Jell-O Gelatin, or 2 or 3 egg whites for a 6-oz. package.

HOW TO CUBE
JELL-O GELATIN
(Pictured on page 80)

Brightly colored cubes that are delicious served alone, with fruits, or in desserts and salads.

**1 package (3 oz.) Jell-O Gelatin
(any fruit flavor)
1 cup boiling water
¾ cup cold water***

*For very firm cubes, cold water may be reduced to ½ cup. For softer cubes, cold water may be increased to 1 cup.

Dissolve Jell-O Gelatin in boiling water. Add cold water. Pour into a shallow pan. Chill until firm—at least 4 hours or overnight. (Cubes hold their shape best when gelatin is chilled overnight.) Then cut in cubes, using sharp knife which has been dipped in hot water. To remove cubes from pan, apply warm wet cloth over bottom of pan; then remove with spatula. Or quickly dip pan in warm water and invert on wax paper. Serve in sherbet glasses with cream or fruit, if desired. Makes 4 servings.

HOW TO FLAKE
JELL-O GELATIN
(Pictured on page 80)

Delicate flakes of Jell-O Gelatin set off fruit or cream beautifully.

**1 package (3 oz.) Jell-O Gelatin
(any fruit flavor)
1 cup boiling water
¾ cup cold water**

Dissolve Jell-O Gelatin in boiling water. Add cold water. Pour into a shallow pan. Chill until firm—at least 4 hours. Break into small flakes with a fork or force through a ricer or large-meshed strainer. Pile lightly in dishes. Top with fruit or ice cream, if desired. Makes 1¾ cups, or 4 servings.

Cream Flakes: Prepare flaked Jell-O Gelatin, folding in 6 to 8 tablespoons light cream before serving.

Fruited Flakes: Prepare flaked Jell-O Gelatin, folding in 1 cup drained fruit.

Peach Melba Sundae: Prepare flaked Jell-O Raspberry Gelatin, using two 3-oz. packages or one 6-oz. package. Spoon gelatin flakes into dishes, making a depression in the middle of each. Drain a 1-lb. can of peach halves; place a peach half, cut side up, in each dish. Top with scoop of ice cream. Makes 5 to 8 servings.

FLAVOR DUETS

Create new Jell-O Gelatin flavors and colors by combining two favorites.

**2 packages (3 oz. each) Jell-O Gelatins (2 fruit flavors—see note)
2 cups boiling water
2 cups cold water**

Dissolve Jell-O Gelatins together in boiling water. Add cold water. Pour into 1-quart bowl, individual molds, or dessert dishes. Chill until firm. Makes 4 cups, or 8 servings.

NOTE: Preferred flavor combinations include lemon with any red flavor, lemon with orange, raspberry with orange, lemon with orange-pineapple, and any two red flavors.

EASY TRICKS

Many special treats can be made with a simple trick or two and easy-to-make Jell-O Gelatin.

Marshmallow Mold: Prepare 1 package (3 oz.) Jell-O Gelatin (any fruit flavor) as directed on package; chill until almost set. Divide 12 diced marshmallows between 4 serving dishes and spoon on gelatin. (Marshmallows will try to pop toward surface.) Makes 4 servings.

Carousels: Prepare any fruit flavor Jell-O Gelatin as directed on package; pour into serving dishes. Chill until almost firm. Then insert several animal crackers into the gelatin around sides of dishes. If desired, insert a thin, red and white striped candy stick or soda straw in center of dish. Chill until firm. Makes 4 servings.

Soft Drink Dessert: Prepare any fruit flavor Jell-O Gelatin, substituting a carbonated soft drink for part or all of the water—use two 6- or 7-oz. bottles or a 12-oz. bottle of cola, ginger ale, root beer, or other soft drink and add water to make up the remainder of the required liquid.

Scalloped Dessert: (Pictured on page 80) Prepare any fruit flavor Jell-O Gelatin as directed on package; pour into sherbet glasses. Chill until firm. Then make scalloped borders around edges by scooping out spoonfuls with a ½-teaspoon measure. Top with prepared Dream Whip Whipped Topping or whipped cream, filling scallops. Garnish with the scooped-out gelatin.

Crown Mold: Prepare two 3-oz. packages or one 6-oz. package Jell-O Gelatin (any fruit flavor) as directed on package. Pour 2 cups gelatin mixture into a 1½-quart crown-shaped or other fancy mold; chill until set, but not firm. Meanwhile, chill remaining gelatin until very thick; then whip until fluffy—see directions on page 84. Pour whipped gelatin over clear gelatin in mold. Makes about 6 cups, or 8 to 10 servings.

Frosted Beverage Glasses: Dampen edge of each glass with a moist, not wet, clean cloth. Dip in Jell-O Gelatin (any fruit flavor), right from package, to coat rim. Use on glasses for soft drinks, milk, or iced tea.

Cut-Outs: (Pictured on page 80) Prepare 1 package (3 oz.) Jell-O Gelatin (any fruit flavor) as directed on package, reducing cold water to ½ cup. Pour into a 9-inch square pan, or to ¼-inch depth in other shallow pans. Chill until firm. Then cut designs, using cutters that have been dipped in warm water. Transfer cut-outs to top of pudding, whipped gelatin squares, or other desserts, using a broad spatula dipped in warm water. If only a few cut-outs are desired, flake remaining gelatin with a fork—see directions on page 85.

Candy Stripe Parfaits: (Pictured on page 80) Prepare 1 package (3 oz.) Jell-O Gelatin (any fruit flavor) as directed on package; chill until very thick. Meanwhile, prepare 1 envelope Dream Whip Whipped Topping Mix as directed on package. Then layer gelatin and prepared whipped topping in parfait or other slender glasses, ending with topping. Chill until serving time—at least 2 hours. Makes about 4 cups, or 6 to 8 servings.

Golden Ring Cupcakes: Prepare two 3-oz. packages Jell-O Lime, Orange, or Orange-Pineapple Gelatin as directed on package; chill until slightly thickened. Drain a 1-lb. 4½-oz. can sliced pineapple; place pineapple slices in bottoms of six 10-oz. baking cups. Cover each with ⅓ cup gelatin and top with a packaged individual sponge cake shell, flat side up. Pour on remaining gelatin. Chill until firm. Makes 6 servings.

TILT-TOP DESSERT
(Pictured on page 80)

A simple dessert with just a touch of creativity to make it different.

> 1 package (3 oz.) Jell-O Gelatin
>   (any fruit flavor)
> 1 cup boiling water
> 1 cup cold water
> 1 cup whipped cream or prepared
>   Dream Whip Whipped Topping

Dissolve Jell-O Gelatin in boiling water. Add cold water. Chill until slightly thickened. Measure and set aside ⅔ cup gelatin. Then fill 4 or 5 stemmed sherbet dishes or small glasses about two-thirds full with remaining gelatin. Tilt glasses so gelatin will set at a slant by catching base between bars of rack and leaning glasses against wall of refrigerator. Chill until firm. Meanwhile, fold whipped cream into ½ cup of the reserved gelatin. Then set glasses upright; fill with cream mixture. Garnish with the remaining clear gelatin. Makes about 3 cups, or 4 or 5 servings.

MULTI-STRIPE DELIGHT

Layers of Jell-O Gelatin form a color spectrum that delights eye as well as palate.

Prepare several fruit flavors of Jell-O Gelatin as directed on packages, using as many packages and flavors as will fill your finest crystal bowl or stemmed glasses—a big brandy snifter was used for the photo. (If capacity of the bowl is unknown, fill it with water; then measure the water and use a 3-oz. package Jell-O Gelatin for each 2 cups required to fill the bowl.)

Layer the flavors in the bowl—see directions for layering Jell-O Gelatin on page 81. If desired, stemmed glasses may be tilted in refrigerator by catching base between bars of rack and leaning top against wall. Chill until firm. Garnish with Frosted Grapes (page 76), if desired. Plan on 4 servings from each 3-oz. package of Jell-O Gelatin used in the bowl.

RECOMMENDED SERVING SIZES OF JELL-O GELATIN MOLDS

TYPE OF MOLD	AVERAGE SERVING
Clear desserts or salads	½ cup
Whipped desserts or salads	¾ cup
Relish salads	⅓ cup
Entree salads	about 1 cup
8-inch pie	6 servings
9-inch pie	7 servings

CHILLING TIMES FOR PREPARING JELL-O GELATIN MOLDS

STAGES	PHYSICAL TESTS	CHILLING TIMES		USES
		Regular Method	Speed-Set Method	
Syrupy	Consistency of thick syrup.	About 1 hour	About 3 minutes	Glaze for sandwiches, pies, and such.
Slightly thickened	Consistency of unbeaten egg whites.	About 1 hour 15 minutes	About 5 or 6 minutes	For adding prepared Dream Whip Whipped Topping or whipped cream, or whipping gelatin with ice bath.
Very thick	Spoon drawn through gelatin leaves a definite impression.	About 1 hour 30 minutes		For adding fruit, vegetables, and other ingredients, or for whipping gelatin without ice bath.
Set, but not firm	Gelatin sticks to finger when touched and mounds or moves to side when tilted.	About 2 hours	About 30 minutes	For adding layers of gelatin.
Firm	Gelatin does not mound or move when mold is tilted and does not stick to finger.	At least 3 hours for individual molds or dishes; at least 4 hours for 2-cup to 1½-quart molds; or at least 5 hours for 2- or 3-quart or deep molds.	About 1 hour	For unmolding and serving.

INDEX

WRITE
FOR SECONDS!

Joys of JELL-O
GELATIN DESSERT

Just send 25¢ and any 6 fruit illustrations
from Jell-O packages with your name
and address (with ZIP code) to: Joys of
Jell-O, Box 1349, Kankakee, Ill. 60901

SEND FOR MOLDS!
[LIMITED OFFER]

Large Ring Mold	**Individual Fluted Molds**	**Individual Ring Molds**	**Tall Crown Mold**
For this 1½-quart copper-tone ring mold, send only $1.25 plus 6 Jell-O package fronts to: Ring Mold Special, Box 3034, Kankakee, Ill. 60901.	To obtain 6 bright aluminum molds, send 75¢, 6 Jell-O package fronts, and your name and address to: Jell-O Molds, Box 3035, Kankakee, Ill. 60901.	For 6 copper-tone molds, send $1.25, 6 Jell-O package fronts, and your name and address to: Individual Ring Molds, Box 3036, Kankakee, Ill. 60901.	Or get a deep 2-quart copper-tone mold — send $1.50, 6 Jell-O package fronts, your name and address to: Tall Crown Mold, Box 3037, Kankakee, Ill. 60901.